Zacharias Tanee Fomum

The way of sanctification

Éditions du Livre Chrétien
4, rue du Révérend Père Cloarec
92400 Courbevoie France
editionlivrechretien@gmail.com

Titre Anglais :

First Edition, 1988 : 15,000 copies.

Second Edition, 1990 : 20,000 copies.

Third Edition, 1992 : 30,000 copies.

Published by :

EDITIONS DU LIVRE CHRÉTIEN

4, rue du Révérend Père Cloarec

92400 Courbevoie - FRANCE

Tél : (33) 9 52 29 27 72

Email : editionlivrechretien@gmail.com

I DEDICATE THIS BOOK TO THE ASSEMBLY IN BEPANDA (DOUALA)

IN GRATEFUL ACKNOWLEDGEMENT OF THEIR LOVE, ENCOURAGEMENT AND SUPPORT IN MANY WAYS OVER THE YEARS

Table of contents

Preface

This book is the fourth in the Christian Way Series. The books in this series are :

Book 1 : The Way of Life

Book 2 : The Way of Obedience

Book 3 : The Way of Discipleship

Book 4 : *The Way of Sanctification*

Book 5 : The Way of Christian Character

Book 6 : The Way of Spiritual Power

Book 7 : The Way of Christian Service

Book 8 : The Way of Spiritual Warfare

Book 9 : The Way of Persecution

Book 10 : The Way of Prayer

Book 11 : The Way of Overcomers

Book 12 : The Way of Encouragement

Book 13 : The Way of Loving the Lord

Book 14 : The Way of Eternal Union

The contents of this book are fundamental. God calls all who are His to a sanctified life. The life of a believer in which sin reigns is subnormal. However, many believers find themselves bound by sin. They are like Lazarus walking out of the tomb with life, but in bondage.

In this book, we have attempted to show as clearly as we can, the way to deliverance from sin. We do not believe that anyone can be as sinless as the Lord Jesus was while in this body of flesh, but this state is already accomplished in the Lord Jesus and therefore, we can be delivered once and for all from the bondage of sin. We also see that this deliverance, though entered into as a crisis, must be maintained daily by a very close walk with the Lord, in full co-operation with Him, by the use of the sanctified mind.

The Psalmist asked, *"How can a young man keep his way pure?"* He provided the answer as follows, *"By guarding it according to thy word. With my whole heart I seek thee, let me not wander from thy commandment! I have laid up thy word in my heart, that I might not sin against thee. Blessed be thou, O Lord; teach me thy statutes! With my lips I declare all the ordinances of thy mouth. In the way of thy testimonies I delight as much as in all riches. I will meditate on thy precepts, and fix my eyes on thy ways. I will delight in thy statutes; I will not forget thy word"* (Psalm 119:9-16).

We believe with him that daily Bible study and prayer (The Quiet Time) is indispensable in maintaining the sanctified life which is first entered into by faith in the finished work of Christ.

Holiness is not just the absence of sin. It includes conformity to God. Sanctification is an aspect of holiness. Our prayer is that the Lord will use this book to work out sanctification in many lives and that many will attain unto *"the holiness without which no one will see the Lord."*

April, 1983.

Zacharias TANEE FOMUM

P.O. Box 6090,

Yaounde - Cameroon.

1

The natural man

We shall approach our study of the way of sanctification by looking at the natural man. The natural man is that one who has not received the Lord Jesus as Lord and Saviour. He is like Lazarus was in the grave - dead.

Man does not become a sinner. He is born a sinner. As a sinner, man has three masters. They are:

1. The world
2. The devil
3. The flesh

He loves the world and the things that are in the world. The devil holds him under control. He practises the deeds of the flesh freely. These include:-

1. Fornication
2. Impurity
3. Licentiousness
4. Idolatry
5. Sorcery
9. Anger
10. Selfishness
11. Dissension
12. Party Spirit
13. Envy

6. Enmity
7. Strife
8. Jealousy
14. Drunkenness
15. Carousing
16. And so on.

He is a slave to these works of the flesh. He may say, for example, that he does not want to fornicate. He may say with his mind that it is wrong but when faced with temptation, his resolutions become impotent and he commits the sin.

Sometimes he may resist sin but this is abnormal. He normally would yield but owing to upbringing and education he may resist for some time, but this resistance soon breaks down. He is himself in sin. Why is this so? It is so because a law called the law of sin and death is operative in him. He is under this law of sin and death and the law must be obeyed. Even if he determines by his own will not to bow to that law, he will nevertheless yield to it.

We can illustrate it this way:-

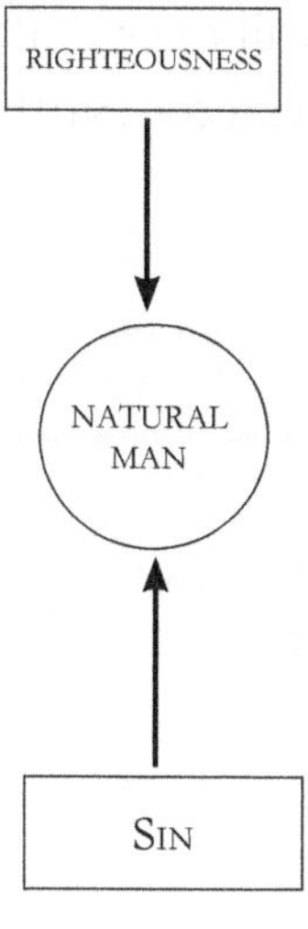

The law of the unregenerate human mind makes some effort to push him upwards but it is no match for the law of sin and death since the mind is darkened

The law of sin and death pushes him down

Because the law of sin and death is operative in the natural man, he will always sink in the direction of sin. There is no pull towards righteousness. He may wish to be righteous but there is no force in him to pull him in the direction of righteousness. Natural man, dead like Lazarus was in the grave, can only decay. Decay is inevitable. A dead man may be preserved from decay by formalin or some other chemical but the preservative will not last long. Its effect will wear out and the person will decay. The works of the flesh are just the odours of a decaying man. How often believers are angry with unbelievers for being this and that and for doing this or that thing! This blaming of the unbeliever is in a sense folly on the part of the believer. Is it normal to blame a corpse for decaying? Would it not be strange if it did not decay? Would we not consider a corpse abnormal if it did not decay? It always decays anyway. Even if the decay of a corpse were not obvious, it would nevertheless remain a corpse. A corpse is a corpse. Who loves even a fresh corpse? Even if a corpse were dressed in very expensive clothes, it would remain an object to be detested. Nothing that is put on a corpse will ever make it into an admirable thing. It will always be detested. Nothing that a natural person does can please God.

2

The carnal believer

THE NEW BIRTH

A corpse will remain a corpse until something is done to it. The corpse cannot do anything to change its condition. Left on its own, it will continue to decay. Lazarus remained in the grave as a corpse until the Lord Jesus did something to it.

The new birth is something supernatural. It is something from above, from God. Man can do nothing to give himself the new birth. It must be done for him. In the new birth God does something for the sinner.

Because of the death of the Lord Jesus Christ on the cross, the life of God is given to the corpse. The corpse is imparted the life of God.

THE STANDING OF THE NEW CREATION

At the moment of the new birth, God imparts to the corpse, the life of God in its totality. In this sense, the new creation possesses all of the life of God. God does not impart His life in small measures. He gives all of it in its totality.

He is the *"once and for all"* sacrifice. The Bible says, *"He abolished the first in order to establish the second. And by that will we have been sanctified through the offering of the body of Christ Jesus once for all"* (Hebrews 10:10). *"And every priest stands daily at his service offering repeatedly the same sacrifices, which can never take away sins. But when Christ had offered for all time a single sacrifice for sins, He sat down at the right hand of God, then to wait until his enemies should be made a stool for his feet. For by a single offering he has perfected for all time those who are sanctified"* (Hebrews 10:11-14). Here the Word of God states that all believers have been sanctified through the offering of Christ. It further states that, by a single offering, Christ perfected for all time those who are sanctified. This means that because of the offering of Christ on the cross, all believers have been:

a. Sanctified

b. Perfected

The sanctification and perfection is once and for all. It can never be repeated.

The Bible continues to say, *"For it was fitting that he, for whom and by whom all things exist, in bringing many sons to glory, should make the pioneer of their salvation perfect through suffering. For he who sanctifies and those who are sanctified have all one origin"* (Hebrews 2:10-11). Again, here the Bible considers all who are true believers as those who are already sanctified.

"So Jesus also suffered outside the gate in order to sanctify the people through his own blood" (Hebrews 13:12). So sanctification was accomplished on the cross, not as something that man did

for himself but as something which Christ did and which is in the believer's past history.

The Bible further says, *"You have been set free from sin and have become slaves of God, the return you get is sanctification and its end, eternal life"* (Romans 6:22).

So the believer has a position before God as one who is entirely sanctified and therefore, positionally, once and for all, entirely sanctified. How can I illustrate this? It is like the son of a king who has all that will make him into a king one day merely by virtue of birth even though he may yet be ignorant of many things.

The Bible says, *"He is the source of your life in Christ Jesus, whom God made our wisdom, our righteousness and sanctification and redemption"* (1 Corinthians 1:30). Christ has already been made the believer's sanctification. From that point of view the believer has already been sanctified.

All this is in the past. It talks of things that have been done and finished with; that can never be repeated and that will never be repeated. God has justified the sinner 100%. There is nothing that the sinner can ever do to add to, improve upon or render more effective, his justification. Before he was condemned, but God carried out his justification and in doing that He left no part of it undone. Nothing can be added to it. In imparting divine nature to the new creation God did it completely.

The experience of the believer

The believer though standing before God as entirely sanctified soon finds that his experience is another thing altogether. He finds that he needs to be entirely sanctified. To this end the apostle Paul wrote to the believers in Thessalonica, "May the God of peace himself sanctify you wholly, and may your spirit and soul and body be kept sound and blameless at

the coming of our Lord Jesus Christ. He who calls you is faithful, and He will do it" (1 Thessalonians 1:23).

So we conclude that there are two aspects to sanctification:-

c. Sanctification already accomplished,

d. Sanctification yet to be accomplished.

In sanctification already accomplished, God has done all that needs to be done and the believer is called to recognize what has been done, enter into it and enjoy it. He is called to know, to reckon and to enjoy what is provided.

In sanctification to be accomplished, God is yet to do something in the believer in order to enable him to conform to the good, the pure and the holy.

In sanctification already accomplished, the new creature in Christ, like the resurrected Lazarus, has God's life in totality even if he is yet bound. In sanctification to be accomplished, God does something in the living Lazarus to render him free from bondage.

In sanctification already accomplished, man contributes nothing. He just enters into what God in Christ has done and begins to enjoy it. He is called upon to see what is his inheritance. He needs revelation and an acting by faith on what God has done.

In sanctification to be accomplished, the Lord expects the believer to actively cooperate with Him in order that he may fully enter his inheritance.

In sanctification already accomplished, God does something for the believer and in the believer, whereas in sanctification yet to be accomplished, God does something in the believer.

THE COMPLETE WORK OF THE CROSS

Before the Lord Jesus died on the cross, He said, *"It is finished."* What He went to do on the cross was accomplished. This finished work included the conquest of the devil. The Bible says, *"Since therefore the children share in flesh and blood, he himself likewise partook of the same nature, that through death he might destroy him who has the power of death, that is, the devil, and deliver all those who through fear of death were subject to life-long bondage"* (Hebrews 2:14-15). Jesus destroyed the devil on the cross. He did this with the purpose of delivering from the chains of the devil, all who were held in the bondage of sin and death.

The Lord did not only destroy the devil. He destroyed his hosts. The Bible says, *"And you who were dead in trespasses and the uncircumcision of your flesh, God made alive together with him, having forgiven us all our trespasses, having cancelled the bond which stood against us with its legal demands; this he set aside, nailing it to the cross. He disarmed the principalities and powers and made a public example of them, triumphing over them in him"* (Colossians 2:13-15). Do you see clearly then what the Lord did? While you were dead in trespasses and sin and the uncircumcision of your flesh, God did the following by the death of Christ:-

1. He made the corpse that you were, alive with Christ.
2. He forgave all your trespasses.
3. He cancelled the bond which stood against you with its legal demands.
4. He cancelled it by nailing it to His cross.
5. He disarmed the principalities and powers.
6. He made a public show of them, showing them as weak and defeated and triumphed over them in total victory.

He did not only do this, He went further. The Bible says, *"And you have come to fullness of life in him, who is the head of all rule and authority. In him also you were circumcised with a circumcision made without hands, by putting off the body of flesh in the circumcision of Christ; and you were buried with him in baptism in which you were also raised with him through faith in the working of God, who raised him from the dead"* (Colossians 2:10-12).

He did the following:-

1. He brought you to fulness of life in Him who is the head of all rule and authority. This means that you have the fulness of life of Christ with His authority over all rule and authority.
2. He circumcised you with a circumcision made without hands.
3. He put off your body of flesh in His circumcision.
4. He caused you to be buried with Him in baptism.
5. 5. He raised you with Himself.

All these were entered into by faith and not by anything that you do.

THE EXPERIENCE OF CARNAL BELIEVERS

Although the Lord has done everything for the believer and although the believer can enter into the full experience of what Christ purchased for him on the cross, most believers do not enter into that fulness.

Why is this so? This is so because of the following reasons:-

1. The *"self"* was crucified but not annihilated. The world was crucified but not removed. The flesh was crucified but not annihilated. The devil was crucified but not removed from the world completely. The legal rights of each of these enemies were removed. Any authority they have is stolen. Their supreme power was taken away. The Lord disarmed the principalities and powers but He did not remove them out of the world. Because these enemies are still present, they are still struggling to see how much authority they can steal for the moment even though they know that their action is illegal and short-lived.

2. The believer can be deceived into thinking that the devil is still in supreme authority and therefore must have the victory. If he is thus deceived, the devil will use this to illegally gain further grounds.

3. The believer can be deceived into ignoring the power that resides in him for overcoming temptation and every work of the devil. A person who has power but does not know that he has it and therefore cannot use it, is in practice, just as helpless

as the one who has no power at all. Look at it this way; Two people are hungry. One has money in his purse but does not know that it is there and therefore does not use it. The other has no money at all. Both of them will starve. The Lord said, *"My people are destroyed for lack of knowledge"* (Hosea 4:6).

4. The believer can be deceived into thinking that because he did not contribute anything towards his salvation, he does not need to contribute anything towards his sanctification. Such thinking which is false, will lead to passivity and the wicked one will exploit such deception.

5. The believer can be blinded from seeing the fact that another law, the law of the spirit of life in Christ Jesus has set him free from the law of sin and death and without this knowledge, he will struggle without success, to overcome sin, by the energy of the flesh.

Because of these reasons, a believer can still sin and live in bondage to the world, the flesh, the devil, self and the law. Such sinning is not a necessary part of Christian experience but it is possible. Believers do sin, although they need not sin. The apostle John wrote, *"My little children, I am writing this to you so that you may not sin"* (1 John 2:1). He however adds, *"But if any one does sin, we have an advocate with the Father, Jesus Christ the righteous"* (1 John 2:1). The believer who still sins and whose life is lived in the energy of the flesh is carnal. He is a spiritual baby even if he believed many years ago. It is for that reason that John writes about sin and the forgiveness of sin to *"little children."*

THE LIFE OF CARNAL BELIEVERS (Romans 7:15-25)

The dominant characteristic of the life of carnality is the *"I"*. The Bible describes that kind of life in Romans 7:15-25. There the Bible says, *"What then shall we say? That the law is sin? By no means! Yet, if it had not been for the law, I should not have known sin. I should not have known what it is to covet if the law had not said,* "You shall not covet." But sin, finding opportunity in the commandment, wrought in me all kinds of covetousness. Apart from the law, sin lay dead. I was once alive apart from the law, but when the commandment, came sin revived and I died; the very commandment which promised life proved to be death to me. For sin, finding opportunity in the commandment, deceived me and by it killed me. So the law is holy, and the commandment is holy and just and good.

Did that which is good, then, bring death to me? By no means! It was sin, working death in me through what is good, in order that sin might be shown to be sin, and through the commandment might become sinful beyond measure. We know that the law is spiritual; but I am carnal, sold under sin. I do not understand my own actions. For I do not do what I want but I do the very thing I hate. Now if I do what I do not want, I agree that the law is good. So then it is no longer I that do it, but sin which dwells within me. For I know that nothing good dwells within me, that is, in my flesh. I can will what is right, but I cannot do it. For I do not do the good I want, but the evil I do not want is what I do. Now if I do what I do not want, it is no longer I that do it, but sin which dwells within me.

So I find it to be a law that when I want to do right, evil lies close at hand. For I delight in the law of God, in my inmost self, but I see in my members another law at war with the law of my mind and making me captive to the law of sin which dwells in my members. Wretched man that I am! Who will deliver me from this body of death? Thanks be to God through Jesus Christ our Lord! So then, I of myself serve the law of God with my mind but, with my flesh I serve the law of sin" (Romans 7:7-25). In this passage,

the word *"I"* (Occurs 40 times)

the word *"My"* (Occurs 8 times)

the word *"Me"* (Occurs 13 times)

40 *"I's"* + 8 *"My's"* + 13 *"Me's"* = WRETCHED MAN

The life of the carnal believer is a life lived in the power of self. The carnal believer may really love the Lord. He may truly want to serve Him. He is often baptized into the Holy Spirit and may have a lot of zeal. The problem with him is that he thinks that he can do many things on his own. He does not quite know himself nor does he know the laws that are operative in him and around him.

THE LAWS OPERATIVE IN THE CARNAL BELIEVER

A. The law of God

The law is of God. It is good. The Bible says, *"The law is holy, and the commandment is holy and just and good"* (Romans 7:12). The law was given not for the believer's undoing but for his good.

The law is spiritual and just. The Bible says, *"We know that the law is spiritual"* (Romans 7:14). *"...that the just requirements of the law might be fulfilled in us"* (Romans 8:4).

The carnal believer acknowledges that the law is good and holy and that God gave it for his good. He loves the law. He says, *"For I delight in the law of God, in my inmost* "self" (Romans 7:22).

When then does that which is God-given become an instrument of the undoing of the carnal believer? The carnal believer says, *"If it had not been for the law, I should not have known sin. I should not have known what it is to covet if the law had not said,* "You shall

not covet" *(Romans 7:7).* "I was once alive apart from the law, but when the commandment came, sin revived and I died; the very commandment which promised life proved to be death to me. For sin, finding opportunity in the commandment, deceived me and by it killed me" (Romans 7:11).

B. The law of sin and death:

There is a law, the law of sin operative in the carnal believer. Nothing good dwells in the flesh of the carnal believer. Something however dwells there, the law of sin. It dwells and is actively operative. Sin is not just an act. It is a law. The Bible says, *"So I find it to be a law that when I want to do right, evil is close at hand"* (Romans 7:22). *"But I see in my members another law at war with the law of my mind and making me captive to the law of sin and death which dwells in my members"* (Romans 7:23). The law of sin and death dwells in the carnal believer.

The law of sin and death ensures that the evil which is near does not remain near but is actually committed. When people sin, they are obeying a law: the law of sin and death. That is the law of sin which rewards those who obey it with death. The law of sin is a powerful law.

C: THE LAW OF THE MIND

There is a law, the law of the mind operative in the carnal believer. The Bible says, *"I see in my members another law at war with the law of my mind..."* (Romans 7:23). The law of the mind is the law of the human will. With this law, wanting very much to keep it, he then makes many resolutions. He says, *"I will not do this again."* I will not talk this way again." "I will not overeat the next time." "I will do things this and that way." The carnal believer uses this law faithfully and sincerely.

There is however a problem. It is this. The law of God is more or less neutral. It states God's position and demand. It says, *"You shall not do this and you shall do this and that."* Having said that, it leaves things to the carnal believer to do as has been said. It does nothing to help him do what must be done. The carnal believer says, *"Yes, what the law of God says is good. I will do it."*

The law of the mind then comes to work and makes right resolutions and plans for carrying out the demands of the Lord. All is set for victory when the carnal believer finds that all his efforts to obey all the law of God all the time, end in failure.

What has happened? Another law that dwells in him and operates in him has come into operation - the law of sin and death. This law of sin and death opposes the law of the mind to ensure that the law of God is not kept. We can illustrate it this way:-

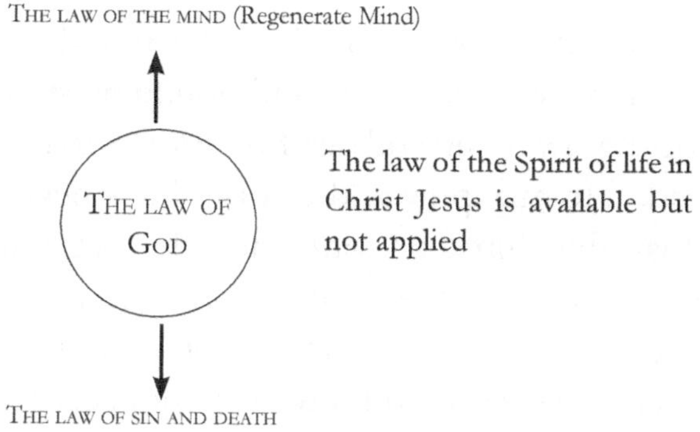

The conflict between the law of the mind and the law of sin and death.

Because the law of sin and death is a far stronger law, it will work in such a way that the carnal believer sins often. Occasionally, he will obey the law of God because of the action of the law of the mind but most of the time the law of sin and death will win.

The carnal believer is often ignorant of these laws at work in himself. It is for that reason that he says, *"I do not understand my own actions. For I do not do what I want, but I do the very thing I hate"* (Romans 7:15). *"I can will what is right, but I cannot do it. For I do not do the good I want, but the evil I do not want is what I do"* (Romans 7:18-19).

He sees the reality of the fact that if he decided not to commit the sin of gluttony, he will make strong resolutions and even while remembering the fact that he should not overeat, will nevertheless overeat and regret it immediately the food has been eaten.

Because of the operation of the law of sin and death, he finds himself a slave, sold under sin and bound by sin to obey the demands of the law of sin and death. He longs to be set free but he is bound. He may pray and fast but he is nevertheless bound. He may find himself confessing the same sin over and over but no sonner is the confession made than he has committed it again and finds himself in total misery. Before he was converted he committed these sins but because he was *"dead"* the light of God did not expose his true condition to him and so he could enjoy sin. Now, the light of God within him exposes sin for what it is and he sees it clearly. He knows the demands of the law of God, knows the desire of his Lord and knows that by sinning he is recrucifying the Saviour who died to save him from sin. He knows all these and would truly want to be pure but he fails over and over and is heart-broken. Think of the horror of knowingly hurting the one person you long with your whole heart to please - the Lord Jesus.

The carnal believer is a very miserable person. He is more miserable than the unbeliever. The unbeliever does not know the conflicts he knows. When the apostle wrote, *"Wretched man that I! Who will deliver me from this body of death?"* (Romans 7:24), he was writing out the cry of many hearts over the years. Do you know such conflicts and cries? Are they your current experiences?

Two pathways are open to the struggling soul at that stage in the development of the spiritual life. He can become discouraged, doubt the fact that he was even saved and allow the devil to take over and cause him to despair completely and walk no more with the Lord, or he can make more efforts in the energy of the flesh. For example, he can decide to increase his:

1. Fasting
2. Praying
3. Bible study
4. Witnessing
5. Giving to the Lord, and so on.

Yes, he can decide to fill his life with one activity after the other in the hope of pleasing the Lord but these activities, though good in themselves, will not lead to the solution of his problem. They are like good drugs but prescribed for the wrong disease. It is like a hungry man who instead of being given food is given a brand new suit. The suit is good and were his problem clothing, it would have served very well. Unfortunately after wearing the suit he will still need food, for that is indeed the problem. All the efforts of the carnal believer are the *"I"*s, *"Me"*s, *"My"*s that will lead to utter failure.

The other pathway is to accept himself as he is and thank God for the situation as it is. That is what the apostle taught. The man cried, ***"Wretched man that I am! Who will deliver me from this body of death?"*** He did not allow the devil to pull him away from the Lord. He did not continue to struggle to keep the law in his own power. He thanked the Lord. He accepted himself. He said, *"Thanks be to God through Jesus Christ our Lord. So then, I or myself serve the law of God with my mind, but with my flesh I serve the law of sin"* (Romans 7:24-25). He needed a Deliverer. God has provided one in the person of the Lord Jesus. The apostle is a child of God. He knows the Lord Jesus as his Saviour from the consequences of sin - hell. He is yet to know Him as the Deliverer from the law of sin and death. Even though he is not yet delivered, for he says, *"So then, I of myself serve the law of God with my mind, but with my flesh I serve the law of sin"* (Romans 7:25), he does not despair. He knows there is a Deliverer. He has not experienced the deliverance but he is confident of the power of the Deliverer. He knows that He cannot fail to deliver him. His situation is not yet normal but it will be normalized. He believes the Lord and thanks Him even though still in bondage. This is great.

Many people would have said to him, *"You are totaly hopeless. You are letting down the Lord by your inconsistent life. How dare you give thanks?"* He however has been led to one truth - Jesus is the Deliverer. He will surely deliver him. The only way to confess his faith in Jesus as the One who will deliver him is to thank God for Him. By that act, he has already taken a big step towards the way of deliverance, for deliverance is in taking Jesus for who He says He is and believing that He has done what He did, then co-operating with Him.

If you are a carnal believer sold under sin, I encourage you to confess with the apostle, *"Thanks be to God through Jesus Christ our Lord! So then, I of myself serve the law of God with my mind, but with my flesh I serve the law of sin."*

You will continue in your present condition for some time but you now know who your Deliverer is:

He is not one philosophy or the other.

He is not one struggle or the other.

He is not despair.

He is not self-blame.

He is not backsliding.

Do not withdraw from the brethren and the world to wait somewhere where some strange thing will happen to you that will suddenly make you into a truly sanctified person. Your Deliverer is the Lord Jesus - the Lord of all glory!

He is willing to deliver you.

He will deliver you.

He has delivered many others who were trapped

just as you are.

He will not make you the exception.

You, look up to Him and then say, *"Thanks be to God through Jesus Christ."* Look up to Him now and say it again and then keep looking up to Him until you are fully delivered. After you are delivered, continue to look up to Him. He is the unchanging answer.

The carnal believer is torn between the desires of the flesh and the desires of the Spirit. Occasionally the desires of the Spirit predominate but most often the desires of the flesh predominate and he is in bondage. Like Lazarus when he came out of the grave, he is bound; he moves but without full freedom. Parts of him are still in bondage. There is conflict in which the desires of the flesh win most of the time. The law of the Spirit of life in Christ Jesus is available in him but he does not co-operate with it because of ignorance or the lack of power to do so.

3

The way of deliverance:

Introduction

As we have already seen, sin is a law and those who are caught within its grip cannot set themselves free. They can try in their own energy but they will fail. Deliverance is possible for all carnal believers. It is provided for in the Lord Jesus Christ. However, deliverance must be preceded by the person coming to the end of himself.

If a carnal believer does not yet see the fact that in his flesh dwells no good thing, he is not ready for deliverance. He will continue to try and even to boast about his achievements. He will try to serve the Lord in the energy of the flesh and may even succeed to produce some results that may deceive him into thinking that he is making progress. God cannot do much for him while he still counts on himself. We emphasize that deliverance is for people who have come to the end of themselves. If you find a man drowning at sea and while he is yet struggling to save himself you try to rescue him, he may cause both of you to drown. The best thing is to allow him to exhaust his own efforts, come to the point of despair and more or less stop trying and then he will let you rescue him.

When a person comes to the end of himself, he will cry out to the Lord Jesus in helpless dependence; he will cry out to Him as one cries to the one and only hope available and the Lord will not fail him. However, to come to that point needs revelation. God must open the eyes of the carnal believer to see the following:-

1. The danger of the life in sin which is death.

"If you live according to the flesh you will die" (Romans 8:13). *"Do you not know that if you yield yourselves to anyone as obedient slaves, you are slaves of the one whom you obey, either of sin, which leads to death, or of obedience which leads to righteousness"* (Romans 6:16). Some think that they can continue in a life of sin and have everything going alright. Some even say, because, *"As one man's trespass led to condemnation for all men, so one man's act of righteousness leads to acquital and life for all men. For as by one man's disobedience many were made sinners, so by one man's obedience many will be made righteous. Law came in to increase the trespass; but where sin increased, grace abounded all the more, so that, as sin reigned in death, grace also might reign through righteousness, to eternal life through Jesus Christ our Lord"* (Romans 5:18-21). With this knowledge some may say that because increased sin gives room for increased manifestation of grace, let them sin so as to offer God an opportunity for more grace flowing and reigning. Such thinking is sad. It is like saying, *"Because sin brought Jesus Christ to earth, let us continue to sin so that God will grant Him to come and abide on earth for ever."* This is utter folly. Anyone who commits sin and is not seriously worried about it is of the devil. He is not a carnal believer. He has never believed! He is a natural man. Let me ask you a personal

question, "Does sin even in its tiniest manifestation bother you and cause you deep anguish of

heart because you are recrucifying the Saviour?" *If not, chances are that you are not a child of God. You belong to your father the devil, for only in his kingdom do people sin and take it lightly. For those who are the children of God, there is a revelation of the dangers of a life lived in sin which is received at the moment of the new birth and as the person begins to walk with the Lord and enters into the conflict with sin, he receives greater revelation about the tragic sinfulness of sin. Has God opened your eyes in an increasing way to see sin for what it is? If not, ask Him.* "Lord open my eyes that I may see sin as You see it."

2. The impossibility of the flesh, struggling on its own, to overcome sin. Unless he sees the fact that man cannot overcome sin and therefore must only hope to be freed from it through deliverance from it, he will not turn wholeheartedly to the Deliverer. He will continue to struggle on his own.

3. The possibility of deliverance.

How can a person turn whole-heartedly to the Deliverer unless he believes that he can be delivered completely? God must open the eyes of the carnal believer to the fact that God is able to sanctify to the uttermost even as He is able to save to the uttermost, all who turn to Him by faith in His Son. Do you believe that total deliverance is found in the Lord Jesus?

4. The joy of the sanctified life.

Some think that a life lived in the sanctification that God provides is boring and unenjoyable. Such thinking is from the Enemy and none who think that way can come into the sanctification of God before a radical change of mind has taken place. God will not lead His children into something which they do not want. He forces no one. All who do not desire the sanctified life will be left where they are. The sanctified life is a life of real blessing. It is the life that God Himself lives. Is it not earth's greatest privilege to be allowed to enter into it? How sad that few desire it with their whole hearts! *"O Lord, open the eyes of Thine children so that they may see!"*

As we are dealing with the need to see, I remember a story recorded in the Old Testament. The Bible says, *"Once when the king of Syria was warring against Israel, he took counsel with his servants, saying, 'At such and such a place shall be my camp.' But the man of God sent word to the king of Israel,* "Beware that you do not pass this place, for the Syrians are going down there." *And the king of Israel sent to the place of which the man of God told him. Thus he used to warn him so that he saved himself there more than once or twice. And the mind of the king of Syria was greatly troubled because of this thing; and he called his servants and said to them,* "Will you not show me who of us is for the king of Israel?" *And one of his servants said,* "None, my lord, O king; but Elisha, the prophet who is in Israel, tells the king of Israel the words that you speak in your bedchamber." *And he said,* "Go and see where he is, that I may send and seize him." *It was told him,* "Behold, he is in Dothan." *So he sent there horses and chariots and a great army; and they came by night, and surrounded the city. When the servant of the man of God rose early in the morning and went out, behold, an army with horses and chariots was round about the city. And the servant said,* "Alas, my master! What shall we do? He said, *"Fear not, for those who are with us are more than those who are with them."* Then Elisha prayed and said, *"O Lord, I pray thee, open his eyes that he may see."* So the Lord opened the eyes of the young man, and he saw and behold the mountain was full of horses and chariots of fire round about Elisha" (2 Kings 6:8-17).

The servant of Elisha passed through the following stages:-

1. He saw the enemy forces at the natural realm.
2. He was taken up with panic.
3. He cried out in despair.
4. Elisha spoke to him, comforted him and prayed that the Lord might open his eyes so that he might see.
5. God opened his eyes; he saw at the spiritual realm and his panic disappeared.

The two armies were always there - the army of the king of Syria which was against Elisha and the army of the Lord which was for Elisha. The army of the Lord was always stronger than the army of the Syrians. For Elisha who saw, there was peace, victory and tranquility. For the servant who saw only at the natural realm there was restlessness. A change came when God opened his eyes, in response to the prophet's prayer and he saw at the spiritual level.

This same principle is applicable to our subject at hand. Those who are already walking in the Spirit have no problem with sin. They have seen and entered into their deliverance. They are like the prophet Elisha. They do not run away from the world to hide in some cave or secluded place in the hope that by so doing they would be separated from sin. They have entered into the full deliverance offered by Jesus and are free even among sinners. They are at peace. Those who are carnal are like the servant of the prophet. They see with the natural eyes their sin and its consequence. They fear, tremble and are ill at ease. They try many things on their own to improve their situation and fail. They should turn to the Lord and ask the Lord to open their eyes so that they may see. When the Lord opens their eyes they will see the wonderful provision of God for sanctified living. They will see the full and perfect deliverance that God has already worked out in the death and resurrection of His Son and they will see how to enter into this holy walk with God which is, after all, the very purpose of Christian election and predestination. The apostle Paul wrote, *"He chose us in him before the foundation of the world, that we should be holy and blameless before Him"* (Ephesians 1:4). *"And you, who once were estranged and hostile in mind, doing evil deeds, he has now reconciled in his body of flesh by his death, in order to present you holy and blameless and irreproachable before him"* (Colossians 1:21-22).

We insist that revelation is necessary. God must open the eyes of the carnal believer to see what He has already done. Without this opening of the eyes, the carnal believer will be led into an intellectual appreciation of the truths of deliverance but be destitute of the experience of sanctification which is the goal of God.

In fact, so much progress in all areas of the Christian walk depends on revelation. Because this is so, the apostle Paul, like Elisha of old never ceased to pray that the eyes of believers would be opened to the reality, not so much of what God will do, but of what God has done. He desired that their eyes might be opened so that they might see and enter into their inheritance which though present was not being enjoyed. In this direction he sometimes prayed that, *"The God of our Lord Jesus Christ, the Father of glory, may give you a spirit of wisdom and of revelation in the knowledge of him, having the eyes of your hearts enlightened, that you may know what is the hope to which he has called you, what are the riches of his glorious inheritance in the saints, and what is the immeasurable greatness of his power in us who believe, according to the working of his great might which he accomplished in Christ when he raised him from the dead and made him sit at his right hand in the heavenly places, far above all rule and authority and power and dominion, and above every name that is named, not only in this age but also in that which is to come; and he has put all things under his feet and has made him the head over all things for the church, which is his body, the fulness of him who fills all in all"*(Ephesians 1:17-23).

He continued to intercede saying, *"That according to the riches of his glory he may grant you to be strengthened with might through his spirit in the inner man, and that Christ may dwell in your hearts through faith, that you, being rooted and grounded in love, may have power to comprehend with all the saints what is the breadth and length and height and depth, and to know the love of Christ which surpasses knowledge, that you may be filled with the fulness of God"* (Ephesians 3:16-19).

God has already done all that is necessary for the believer's deliverance from sin. Each believer must see what has been done and enter into it. What God has yet to do is to open believer's eyes to see what He has done. For that He needs the co-operation of those believers that have experienced deliverance and are walking in it. The prayer of Elisha led to the opening of his servant's eyes so that he could see. Paul prayed that believers might see. In the case of Lazarus, the Lord gave him life, but for his total freedom, He needed the co-operation of those who were alive and free, for it was to them that He said, *"Unbind him and let him go"* (John 11:44).

All who have entered into the life of sanctification must pray that the Lord will open the eyes of those who, though alive are yet bound by sin, to see that their deliverance has been provided for. The more there are sanctified and praying saints in the Church, the more the carnal believers will readily pass

from carnality into holy living. This means that a spiritual babe born into a church that is filled with carnal believers will remain in carnality much longer than if he were born into a local church where many of her members had already entered into the sanctified life.

Do you then see why God is reluctant to add members to a carnal, sin-loving local church? Do you then see why the first responsibility of the church is to render herself holy even as her Lord before it can make evangelism and church planting supreme goals?

In the natural realm, sick people have a reduced capacity of reproduction. If they reproduce, they will tend to reproduce sick children. Their true nature is revealed in their offsprings. Look at your spiritual children. They say something about you. If they are non-existent, you are dangerously sick. If they are feeble, you are playing with sin somewhere. If they are strong and Christ-like, that is indicative of your walk with the Lord.

For the sake of the glory of the Lord; for the sake of the type of children who must be born into the kingdom of God and who to some extent will resemble you, I exhort you to have your eyes opened by the Lord so that you may enter into the deliverance from sin that He has provided for you.

4

The way of deliverance - 1 :

KNOWING

IDENTIFICATION WITH CHRIST IN HIS DEATH :

There is a pertinent question which every believer ought to ask himself. It is this, *"How did I become a sinner?"* The answer is very obvious. I became a sinner by birth. If I were never born into the world, I would never be a sinner. Or, if I were born into the world as a goat or cow or chicken, I could live and have no problem with sin. But I am not a goat. I am a human being. I was born into sin - born with it. I was born into Adam. When Adam sinned, I became a sinner. I do not have to do any other thing to become a sinner. My origin makes me a sinner. From birth all human beings are sin-ners. Each human being begins his human life with a sin nature - dead in sin.

Having got into Adam by birth and by getting into Adam, I got into sin, the next question, that arises is, *"How can I get out of sin? How can I cease to be a sinner?"* The answer is obvious. To get out of sin, to cease to be a sinner, you have to get out of Adam. All who are out of Adam are out of sin. The question then is, *"How can I who was born into Adam get out of him into whom I was born?"* The answer is, *"I can get out of Adam by death."* There is no other way. All struggles and efforts at reformation will not change my fundamental nature while I remain in Adam. Death will settle it in a beautiful way and settle it once and for all.

Christ did that for me. He did that for all human beings. The Bible says, *"But God shows his love for us in that while we were yet sinners Christ died for us"* (Romans 5:8). His blood atoned for all of our sins :

all our past sins,

all our present sins and

all future sins.

Yes, Christ died for us. He died for me, Zach Fomum, and He died for you, whatever your name may be.

Christ did not only die for us. We were included in that death. The Bible says, *"Our old man was crucified with him"* (Romans 6:6). *"We have died with Christ"* (Romans 6:8).

We ask, *"Did Christ die for us?"* The emphatic answer is, *"Yes, Christ died for us"* We ask again, *"Did we die with Christ?"* That same emphatic answer comes through, *"YES, We died with Christ."* Let me make it more personal. *"Did Christ die for you?"* The answer must be, *"Yes Christ died for me."* I then ask another question *"Did you die with Christ?"* The same *"YES,"* must be the answer.

You may not be too sure but the same Bible that says that Christ died for you, also says that you died with Christ. If the first statement is true, then the second one is true also. If you believe the first statement, you have to believe the second one. If you doubt the second statement, you should doubt the first one too. Both statements are given to you in the same packet. You cannot accept one and reject the other. You have a choice of either accepting or rejecting both. The apostle Paul confessed, *"I have been crucified with Christ"* (Galatians 2:20). You too should confess, *"I have been crucified with Christ."*

When the Lord Jesus Christ died on the cross, He was crucified as the last Adam. The first Adam brought total damage to the whole race and to the whole world. Jesus, as the last Adam, gathered all that was in the first Adam in Himself and as He went to the cross, He took it all with Him and brought it all to an end on that cross.

You and I, were included in that *"wiping out"* that took place on that historic day on the cross. From God's point of view, and that is the only point of view that really matters, all of the old creation was summed up in Christ Jesus and by His death on the cross, He brought it all to an end. There is a sense in which the Father of all glory does not see the old creation as still existing. There is a sense in which it can pose no problem to Him because He settled it once and for all on the cross and finished it there. When the Lord Jesus said from the cross that it was finished, in a sense He meant that all of the old creation was finished.

This does not only apply to the *"bad"* things that were in the first Adam. The *"good"* things were also included. All that is natural, that is Adam - natural goodness, natural kindness, natural talents like : eloquence

beauty

a strong will

tenderness

and the rest

were dealt away with because they were of the first Adam. That is why anyone who tries to serve God on the basis of these things and with them, will fail. God sentenced all natural goodness and natural talents to death on the cross. Often people say, *"O, this man is so gifted. I wish he were a Christian so that he could use his talents for God!"* This is sheer foolishness because such thinking hopes that natural talents can serve in the Kingdom of God. They cannot be of use to the Lord. People with natural talents will depend on their talents and not on the Lord and God wants to use only people who depend on Him entirely. Some brethren even go on to say; *"This person is so naturally good. He needs only a small push and he will be in the Kingdom."* This is not so, for such people will display their *"goodness"* before God and say, *"I fast twice a week, I do this and that thing,"*and they will hardly fall humbly before the Lord and cry out, *"Lord, be merciful to me, sinner that I am."* At the other extreme of it is the thinking by some brethren that people in great physical need will respond most readily to the gospel since they hardly have anything in the world. This thinking too is not correct. Once we held an evangelistic meeting among handicapped people in our city. We first invited them to a meal and after that we proceeded to proclaim the gospel to them. One of the first people to go out in protest was a man who was so lame that he walked on all fours like an animal. When he walked out many young brethren were surprised. Now they understand better. Human gifts or human need cannot give a person standing before God or access to God. The Lord Himself must do it. That is why the Lord Jesus went to the cross. All that was in the first Adam is useless to God and useless in the building of the Kingdom of His Son.

Brothers and Sisters, let me insist humbly but boldly that when the Lord Jesus died on the cross, you too died. You were done with. You

were ruled out. You are ruled out! You are finished. All that pertains to the old man in you has been brought to an end and settled. The *"self"* you loathe so much was put on the cross with Christ. You are free from that *"self"*. You are free from sin. The Bible says, *"He that is dead is free from sins"* (Romans 6:7). Because you died with Christ on the cross, you are free from sin. Your old man was crucified with Christ. It can never be otherwise. Your crucifixion can never be made effective by your will or by any efforts of the flesh but only by accepting what Christ did on the cross. Your eyes must be opened to the finished work of Christ on the cross. Without that, you will not know freedom from the power of sin. Man's way of dealing with sin is to try and conquer or suppress it by deceiving himself that, because it has been temporarily put under control, it is dealt away with. That is like a person who stands on the head and tail of a big viper and then makes as if the viper is dead. Of course the viper is not dead. It is very much alive. While the person exerts a lot of pressure, he may keep it under control but when his legs give way and he can no longer exert a lot of pressure on the viper, it will get away and be free to cause havoc. Many of God's children say, "If only I had been stronger, I would not have committed this sin; if only I prayed more, I would overcome this and that sin. I am frequently overcome by this particular sin. I must fast in order to overcome it." *Fasting, prayer, and all else are good but they are not the answer to sin. The Bible nowhere asks believers to overcome sin. No one can overcome sin. The Bible way is first of all through knowing what Christ did on the cross. The Bible answer to the believer's problem with sin is,* "We know that our old self was crucified with Him, (Christ) so that the sinful body might be destroyed and we might no longer be enslaved by sin" *(Romans 6:6).* "Do you see what it says?" It says, we know that:-

1. Our old self was crucified with Him.
2. So that our sinful bodies might be destroyed.
3. So that we might no longer be enslaved to sin.

God's answer starts with revelation knowledge of what He did in Christ. God's way of dealing with sin is not to attack the sin but the sinner. He took the sinner to the cross and crucified him there so that the sinner's sinful body might be destroyed; so that that body might no longer be enslaved by sin. Yes, God took the sinner to the cross. No one ever goes to the cross and escapes death, for the cross makes no compromises. It negotiates nothing. It does not rest until its victim is dead. If you went to the cross with Christ and the Bible states clearly that you did then your old self was surely crucified as the Bible states. Maybe you think that God should have acted differently. Maybe you think that God should have spared the sinner the cross and instead helped him to get rid of the old man by strengthening his natural will. This would not have worked. It might have provided some temporary solution but God is interested in lasting solutions and that is why He chose the way of the cross.

THE DEAD MAN DIED

Before you came to Christ, you were dead in trespasses and sins. On the cross you were dead, you were crucified with Christ. Therefore we can legitimately say that The dead man died. You have died twice. You are twice dead and because you are a child of God you are twice born. God has provided in the death of His Son on the cross, His one way by which twice dead men can become doubly alive to the glory of God.

That is why all who embark on overcoming the flesh through self- struggles are inevitably doomed to fail. They have already failed. The cross of Christ proclaims a message of total failure for them.

Those who will walk in freedom from the power of sin must accept God's facts. Those facts say, *"Your old self was crucified."* You may not feel it but it is true. You may not understand it but it is true. Your experience may contradict it but it is true. Maybe the Enemy is causing you to doubt God's Word. He told Eve, *"You will not die,"* when God had said that she would die. She believed him, and ate the fruit and became a slave to the devil and died. God's Word stands true. Believe it. The Enemy may be telling you even now, *"God has said that your old self was crucified. But look at yourself. Look at your experience. You have just done this and that. Is that evidence of death with Christ? Do not be stupid. At least be honest and say that you are fully alive."* Yes, the devil may point your experience to you and say, *"That is reality. Believe it."* Do you not see the hand of the Tempter and Deceiver in that? Can God's Word be false and the Enemy's word true? Which is more dependable? Your feelings or God's Word? If you want to please God, you must walk by faith and not by sight. Faith believes God's

Word 100% even if there were a billion things to challenge it. If you would know God's sanctification, you must believe that His Word is true and that nearly two thousand years ago, your old man was crucified with Christ on the cross. So the Bible says, *"We know that our old man was crucified with Christ."* We know! We know!! We know!!! Now a big question arises and it is addressed to you, *"Do you know?"* The question is not whether or not God had done it, for He has surely done it. The problem is not with God. The question is *"Do you know?"* Without this knowledge, deliverance from sin is impossible.

As we said earlier, God must open the believer's eyes to see and his mind to know. His eyes must be opened to see the Lord Jesus as crucified and he with Him and his mind must be enlightened to know that that co-crucifixion is God's answer to the problem of sin. Merely knowing it theoretically will not make much sense. May God reveal it to you! Too many of God's children *"know"* too much of their sin and their sinful nature. They confess it night and day. But oh, for a revelation of the finished work on the cross!! It was done by God there, on that cross, 2000 years ago and it was done for you. Why don't you pray now and say, *"O Lord, open my eyes that I may see that you settled it all on the cross?"*

You are dead with Christ. You are crucified with Christ. Your experience may say a different thing but God says you have been crucified. He knows best. He must be right. He is right. Make up your mind now whom you are to believe. Either God and His Word or you and your experience. The choice will determine how much progress you can make. If you *"know"*, you can make progress. If you doubt, or do not know, you are stuck. You cannot progress.

Many believers are often saying to the Lord *"Lord, crucify me, crucify me."* They seem to be saying, *"Lord Jesus, go to the cross again. This time take me along with you. I will surely come along this time. When you went to the cross for the first time, I was not ready, now I am ready. Let us go there now so that I can be crucified with you."* Brethren, is this right? How can Christ crucify you again when He has already done so? How can He go to the cross again when He has been there once and for all? Have you ever tried to put on a dress which you already have on for a second time? It is clumsy, is it not? It is impossible, is it not? There is so much time spent praying that Christ might do that which He has already done and which He cannot repeat. How will you like it if the Lord Jesus says now, *"I will come down to earth from my glory and go to the cross a second time for these children of mine who find some things difficult?"* He has been there once and for all.

If the government of this nation wanted to deal with the problem of lung cancer caused by the smoking of cigarettes and the like, it could do one of three possible things. It could train and employ many doctors and technicians to diagnose and treat the diseases that are found, but this will obviously be the poor way out because all the diseases may not be diagnosed, and some that are diagnosed will not be treated and the patients will die. The government could on the one hand, ban the smoking of cigarettes. This may be effective within the measure that people take the ban seriously. However, those who are too powerless to resist will smoke in hiding and end up with the disease. The last possibility is that the government could ban the existence of the cigarette factories. This last measure will be effective because the problem would have been handled at the source. Some people might still stock up cigarettes to smoke in the days ahead but that would not go on indefinitely. It will come to an end. From the moment that a presidential decree bans the cigarette factories, you can be sure that the future of cancer caused by smoking in the nation is permanently settled. The presence of even many cartons of cigarettes will not bother anyone who knows that the decree has been passed by authority that cannot be challenged or disobeyed.

When the Lord Jesus died on the cross and took all humanity with Him, the future of sin in the lives of believers was settled permanently. There is a sense in which the sins of His children cause no anxiety to the Lord. Do you know that? God is so sure of the death of Jesus on the cross and the co-death of all His adopted children with Him that He lives in undisturbed peace even when few in the church are apparently making rapid progress in the school of sanctification.

IDENTIFICATION WITH CHRIST IN HIS RESURRECTION

Good as union with Christ in His death is, this is not final. Death is not final, for if it were, it would have resulted in the elimination of the old man with no possibility of a new man. God was interested in something more than the elimination of the old man. His goal was a new humanity and death was just a part of the process leading to the acquisition of this new humanity. This brings us to identification with Christ in His resurrection. The Bible says, *"If we have been united with Him in a death like his, we shall certainly be united in a resurrection like his"* (Romans 6:5). *"You were raised with Him through faith in the working of God"* (Colossians 2:12).

So, when Jesus went to the cross, He took you with Himself and by your death with Him brought all of the old man to an end. After His death there was a resurrection and again the Lord Jesus took all who died with Him into His resurrection. This opens up the possibility of people living in vital fellowship with Him in newness of life, where sin has no dominion. However, before we talk some more on His resurrection and our identification with Him in it, let us see what happened between His death and His resurrection.

Between these two great events was His burial. The Lord Jesus who died on the cross was buried. In a sense, the Lord waited for the burial to take place before He could resurrect. What stands for burial? Baptism does. It would have been abnormal for the Lord to have died and refused to be buried. In fact, if He had said, *"Do not bury me"* He would have also have been saying, *"I am not dead"*, for dead people do not protest. They submit. The Lord Jesus did not protest. He submitted. He let God decide that that body had to be buried. God did not exempt even Christ from burial. He exempts no one from burial (Baptism today).

When Christ died, we died with Him. We act out our death with Him by repentance towards God and faith in the Lord Jesus. Christ was buried. We act out our burial with Him by submitting to baptism (Immersion). We go right under water and are totally covered up with water even as He was totally covered up in the grave.

We are baptized into Christ. We are baptized into His death (Romans 6:3). We are not baptized into someone else or into some religious system. If it is Biblical baptism, it must be into Christ and into His death. The Bible says, *"We were buried with*

Him by baptism into death" (Romans 6:4). When a person is buried, it is a final seal that he is indeed dead. Baptism into the death of Christ also says that our union into His death is a settled matter.

When a man is buried, all the hopes that people had in him are damaged permanently. For that person, his own hopes of gain and success in the world are also buried permanently. The apostle Paul puts it all very clearly. He says *"But far be it from me to glory except in the cross of our Lord Jesus Christ, by which the world has been crucified to me and I to the world"* (Galatians 6:14).

Do you see something? It is this: Those who have died with Christ and been buried with Him have been brought to an end with regards to all that pertains to their old life. In that death the works of the old man - of the flesh - which include :- fornication, impurity, and so on as we saw in the first chapter, were brought to an end, for when a man dies, his activities die with him. Take for example, a man who through theft brought misery to an area. When he dies that area immediately knows rest. For him to be dead and still be stealing is abnormal.

All who died with Christ died to the deeds of darkness and to all the desires of the flesh.

The second Adam

Christ died as the last Adam. However, He is also the second Adam. As the second Adam, the Lord Jesus through the resurrection, became the Head, the starting point of a new race. This new race is called Christians, that is, those who are in Christ and in whom Christ is.

God has made you one with Christ in His resurrection. He has put you into His resurrection life and thereby put you into the new race, the new humanity. You see, God does not look at you as an American, a German, an Ewondo, a Bamilike or a man from Bafut. All these boundaries, separations and distinctions belong to the old creation. He looks at you as belonging to the new race - Christians. The Bible says that in Christ *"There cannot be Greek or Jew, Circumcised, Barbarian, Scythian, Slave, free man, but Christ is all and in all"* (Colossians 3:11). In the light of this, to be bound by tribal, national, racial, regional barriers is to proclaim a sad message which says, *"I am still bound to the old life with its inclinations and prejudices,"* and this is a shame. But thanks be to God! We are free from these barriers. The new humanity is a stark reality.

Yes, we were buried with Him.

We are resurrected with Him.

We have come to fulness of life in Him.

We are enthroned with Him.

These are God's facts. They are God's realities. He has called us into them. He has put us into them. Glory be to His Holy Name!

Being in the new humanity means that you have come to life. You are indeed alive. You are alive with God's new life. Before Christ was crucified; before God put you into His death and resurrection, you were dominated by the old life and its decay. Now a new principle of life has been put into you. You are alive, not with the old life but with a brand new life that is radically different from the past one. That is what has taken place in you. That is what you are. God has done it. The question is, *"Do you know that He had done that in you and for you?"*

You can put off the old man because you have a new life in you that is different from the old one. You can put on the new man because you are alive, fully alive with the Lord Jesus and in the Lord Jesus.

THE POTENTIALS OF THE NEW MAN

When the Lord resurrected from the dead, there was continuity and discontinuity with His former body. There was continuity in that He could be recognized. There was discontinuity in that unless He revealed Himself, even those who were close to Him in His life before His death and resurrection could not recognize Him. Mary Magdalene could not recognize Him until He

called out to her. The disciples on the way to Emmaus could not recognize Him until He broke bread and gave them.

There will be something about the new man resurrected in the Lord Jesus, that people will find impossible to understand.

The risen Lord could pass through walls, appear and disappear. This He did not do before the resurrection. This tells us that God has put enormous power in the new creation. There is power available for those who are risen in Christ to completely put off the old man and to completely put on the new man. It is possible, because of union with the Lord Jesus in His death and resurrection, to terminate radically with sin in all its forms and manifestations and to put on Christ in the totality of His character.

We shall continue in this book to look at that aspect of sanctification that has to do with total deliverance from sin and in the next book, *"The Way of Christian Character,"* we shall concentrate on the putting on of the character of Christ.

This is all possible for you as a child of God. It is indeed possible. However, the question remains: *"Do you know that it is possible? Do you know that the power of God resides in you and is available for you to succeed, Jesus helping you?"*

Do you know? Do you know?? Do you know??? If you know, you can go on to the next step and on to full liberty! God bless you!

5

The way of deliverance - 2 :

RECKONING

We have said that the first step to deliverance from sin is *"knowing"*. We said that this *"knowing"* was something beyond just a mental acknowledgement of facts. It is the *"knowing"* that comes when the Lord opens the eyes and one can see what God has already done in Christ Jesus for and in the believer.

However, knowing is only the first step. There is a second step. It is Reckoning. The Bible says to those who *"know"*, *"So you must reckon yourselves dead to sin and alive to God in Christ"* (Romans 6:11).

If a person is to reckon, that one needs to know clearly what reckoning means. Reckoning is the act of recording facts. It is to put accounts down. Accounts are based on facts. If someone gives me one thousand francs, I must record one thousand francs. If I give someone one hundred francs from the one thousand francs then my accounts must show that I have nine hundred francs. Accounts are a very exact science.

The word *"Reckon"* or *"Reckoned"* or *"Reckoning"* is used in the following places in the Bible. The Bible says of Abraham, *"And behold, the word of the Lord came to him,* "This man shall not be your heir; your own son shall be your heir." *And he brought him outside and said,* "Look toward heaven, and number the stars, if you are able to number them." *Then he said to him,* "So shall your descendants be." "And he believed the Lord, and he reckoned it to him as righteousness" (Genesis 15:4-6).

"For if Abraham was justified by works, he had something to boast about, but not before God. For what does the Scripture say? "Abraham believed God, and it was reckoned to him as righteousness." *Now to one who works, his wages are not reckoned as a gift but as his due. And to one who does not work but trusts him who justifies the ungodly, his faith is reckoned as righteousness"* (Romans 4:2-5).

We can say that Abraham believed God's facts even when his experience was not yet in conformity to those facts and God reckoned the facts as real for him in His record. *"We say that faith was reckoned to Abraham as righteousness"* (Romans 4:9). Abraham had faith and in his records it was written *"righteousness"* The account was correct. It was accurate. To reckon is to record. To reckon God's facts is to record God's facts. Now that we know what reckoning means we can ask the question, *"What are we to reckon?"* We are to reckon God's facts about us and those facts say that, *"We are dead to sin and alive to God in Christ."*

We are dead to one thing - sin.

We are alive to one person - God.

One person has made this possible - Jesus

Christ.

In Christ then, you are dead to sin. In Christ you are alive to God. We can put it this way. In union with Christ you are dead to sin and in union with Christ you are alive unto God: alive for God's purposes, alive for God's use.

We can say, that in union with Christ you died to sin and you are dead to sin. It happened when Christ took you with Him to the cross nearly two thousand years ago and it stands good today. Also you became alive to God two thousand years ago and God has not changed His mind about it. It stands today as it stood then. It is as good now as it was then. At that time when He took you with Himself to the cross, you were dead in trespasses and sins, yet He did it. Now irrespective of your spiritual condition, what He did still holds good.

So, record, reckon, write down accurately, *"I am dead to sin and alive to God in Christ."* Why can I write this down so confidently? Am I not deceiving myself since my experience or recording is based not on what I feel but on what I know and what I know is not the facts of my experience but God's facts. *"We know"* precedes *"We reckon"* and that puts things in order.

So, our *"reckoning"* is based on God's facts which are the most exact facts and those exact and unchanging facts are, *"We know that our old self was crucified with him so that the sinful body might be destroyed, and we might no longer he enslaved by sin, for he who has died is free from sin"* (Romans 6 : 6-7). Because these are God's facts, we can record or write them down accurately, without fearing that we are being mistaken. Moreso, we reckon all these facts (in Christ,*" for God has put us in Christ and what happened to Christ has happened to us. If it were not* "in Christ," *there would be no hope for us. It it were* "in X," where X stands for some :-

philosophy

doctrine

religion

denomination

personality or any other, it would be groundless and therefore be self-deception. But thanks be to God, it is all, *"in Christ."* What a sure foundation!

In reckoning, it is as if God is saying to us, *"I put you into Christ. You died in Him. You were buried in Him. You rose with Him. You are enthroned with Him. Now I want you to take account of these things. Write them out in your life. Write them down in your life. They are exact. They are exact. They are true. If you see something in your character or actions that seems to contradict My facts, refuse that thing; refuse that experience because it is from the Enemy. Whatever contradict My facts are the Enemy's lies. You are not to base your life on the Enemy's lies. You are to base it on My facts. Therefore you are to write out My facts and believe them even in the midst of the worst failure. Even in the midst of that experience, My facts remain true. They do not depend on you. They depend on Me and they depend on what My Christ went through and I am the Lord that never changes. Your changing experience cannot change My unchanging facts. Believe in me. Believe My facts."*

God does not only ask us to reckon. He compels us to do so. It is a command. His Word says, *"So you must reckon..."* There is no choice in the matter. Whether you like it or not, He calls you to it. Whether you feel it or not, He calls you to reckon.

Whether your experience conforms to it or not, you are to reckon. You must reckon or be living in total disobedience.

There is a sense in which the one who wants to base his reckoning on his experience is specially foolish. The Bible says reckoning precedes the experience of that which is reckoned. Let us put it this way :

KNOWING ⊠ RECKONING ⊠ YIELDING ⊠ DELIVERANCE ⊠ EXPÉRIENCE

Experience is at the end. Reckoning must come before experience. God has decreed that order and that being His order, it is the way in which it will work. If someone wants to experience before he reckons, he will remain in perpetual failure and ever cry, *"O wretched man that I am, who will deliver me from this body of death?"* This is so because to say that, he must be prepared to give up his own thoughts and plans and ways of deliverance for those of the Lord Jesus.

The one who says that he needs the experience of deliverance first in order to reckon, is like a man in a dark room. The room has electricity and he knows where the switch is. He is told to put on the switch in order that he may have light. He can do it but he instead says, *"I must have light before I can put on the switch."* As long as he maintains that way of thinking and acting, he will remain n darkness; for light will never come before he has put on the switch. That is where faith comes in; for someone may say, *"Let me not make a fool of myself. I may put on the switch and there is no light and I will look light a fool."* Well, there is a big choice. There is a big choice between your thinking and God's Word. You choose what you want. There is another thing! Are you prepared to stake your life on the promises of God? Are you prepared to say, *"I believe him. I will act as He has promised. If His Word fails, I want to fail with Him"*? if you are not prepared for that, you cannot go far with Him, for "Without faith it is impossible to please God

Brother, Sister, you are dead to sin and alive to God in Christ. Whether you like it or not, whether you feel it or not, it is true because God has done it. He has done it in Christ. What is your name?

- Elizabeth?
- Paul?
- Stephen?
- Ruth?

I command you in the name of the Lord Jesus to take up your pen and write on the front page of your Bible, "*...[Your name] IS DEAD TO SIN AND ALIVE TO GOD IN CHRIST.*" Never doubt the fact. It is settled in heaven. It can never be unsettled. Christ said, *"It is finished. He again says now that you have done it,* "It is finished." *God says,* "Amen" *to that transaction. Do you echo that* "Amen"*? I ask again,* "DO YOU ECHO THAT *'AMEN'* "?

If you do, then why don't you stop now and thank God that it is so? Why don't you turn to rejoicing in Him because of it? If you do, blessed are you!

This is the essence of faith. It is the assurance of things hoped for. It is the evidence of things not yet seen. Without faith it is impossible to please God, and faith is the accepting and the believing of God's facts.

We reckon by faith. We believe God's fact by faith, even while we are still in the midst of temptation and possible failure. As we turn our eyes from ourselves and our failures and look at the Lord Jesus and reckon His facts about us, we are brought to experience those facts. Glory be to the Lord!

If we so reckon, yield, accept God's deliverance and co-operate with the law of the spirit of life in Christ Jesus, it will be impossible for sin to reign in our mortal bodies. We will be able to experience the injunction,

"Let not sin therefore reign in your mortal bodies, to make you obey their passions" (Romans 6:12).

How do we not let sin reign? We do not prevent sin from reigning by fighting, but by reckoning. It is not by suppressing but by reckoning. It is not by all other human efforts, but by reckoning. Again, I feel like shouting aloud, *"Glory be to the Lord! Glory, glory, glory to His Holy Name!"*

We do not only reckon ourselves dead but we also reckon ourselves alive to God. You are alive unto God! God is no longer dealing with a corpse but with a living being. He is dealing with one who is alive from the dead and one who is alive unto God – to serve God, to do His will and to accomplish all that satisfies His heart. He is dealing with one who will communicate with Him and get to know the desires of His (God's) heart even if they are only felt in the heart of God and are not written or spoken out.

Is that not wonderful? Some time back I thought it was presumptuous to nurse such hopes in any heart, but thanks be to God, He has placed such hopes and desires in our heart

Himself and He is at work in us both to will and to do His good pleasure. That is victory!

6

The way of deliverance - 3 :

YIELDING

To the one who knows and who reckons, the Bible demands that he yields. It is possible to yield to the wrong person and to the wrong things and it is possible to yield to the right person and to the right things The Bible says,

"Do you know that if you yield yourself to any one as obedient slaves you are slaves of the one you obey, either of sin, which leads to death, or of obedience which leads to righteousness?" (Romans 6:16).

The Bible goes on to insist that yielding to the wrong things must not be allowed. It says

"Le not sin therefore reign in your mortal bodies, to make you obey their passions. Do not yield your members to sin as instruments of wickedness, but yield yourselves to God as men who have been brought from death to life, and your members to God as instruments of righteousness" (Romans 6:12-16).

Yielding means that we establish a throne on our hearts and enthrone a king and become the servants or rather, the slaves of that king. It means that we make a commitment to obey Him all the time. There is only one king who should be enthroned by those who have *"known"* and *"reckoned"*. That one is King Jesus.

So we are to yield to God. We are to surrender to Him. When driving on a minor road, on approaching a major road, the sign *"YEILD,"* is often seen. That sign means that the one on the minor road must stop. In yielding, as my will which is the *"minor"* will approached the will of God which is the major will, the *"minor"* will stops so that the major will may operate. The Bible says,

"Yield yourselves to God as men who have been brought from death to life, and your members to God as instruments of righteousness" (Romans 6:19).

So we yield to God. We are separated from Him. We are apart to belong exclusively to Him and to be used exclusively by Him. This is the meaning of holiness or sanctification. Anyone who is set apart in

spirit

soul

body

to be God's exclusive property and to be used exclusively by Him is a holy person. That one submits himself totally to God so that God monopolizes him absolutely.

So yielding means that I make myself His completely: 100%. My spirit, soul, body and all are abandoned to Him without reserve and without regret. My gifts, my talents my possessions, and all are given to him without condition. Yielding means that from the moment I am yielding, my sole concern in life becomes the knowing and the accomplishing of His will. Whatever His will is, it is accepted gladly. If that will keeps me at the University as His Ambassador there, I gladly accept it with joy. If that will keeps me in Cameroon, I accept it with joy. If it sends me to another country, I gladly say, *"Yes, ma Lord."* If that will makes me minister to multitudes from the stage, I accept it gladly. If on the other hand, that will sends me to a mountain place to spend to spend the rest of my life in a ministry of intercession, unknown to men, I accept it with joy and without reserve. I am willing to be *"Great"* or *"Small"* I am willing to be *"Known or Unknown"*. Yieldedness means that I surrender all of my rights to determine anything and have anything. I refuse to choose. I accept where He puts me. It may be comfortable or uncomfortable. It may be pleasant on unpleasant. It may be *"good"* as seen by men. I do not care about these considerations. I ask only one question, *"Is it His will?"* If the answer is *"Yes,"* then the issue is settled. I must submit to it and carry it out with joy.

This is what being a slave means. Take my house servant for example. He is my servant and not my slave. He can say to me today, *"It is finished. I will serve you no more."* From that moment, I can no longer force him to stay. He is free. He must do what He wants. He can go. But if he were my slave, he would never have a choice. He would serve me all the time. He will set aside his own will. When I am hard, he will serve me. When I am nice and tender, he would serve me. The slave has only one operative will – His master's.

In yielding ourselves as the Lord's slaves, we become slaves of righteousness (Romans 6:18). We are slaves of God

(Romans 6:22). Our reward is (sanctification) which is the special privilege of serving Him exclusively to Him. This is slavery, yet what a wonderful kind of slavery which ends in eternal life.

We have said something about yielding. We have seen that the Word of God demands that we yield our bodies. We must settle very clearly which bodies are to be yielded for if I am to yield my body, I must be clear about the body involved. Which body am I to yield? Is it my old body, the one I inherited from Adam? Is it the old body beset and bound by sin, disobedient and rebellious? No! That body, the old body was yielded in Christ unto death. God does not want to have it in His service.

The body that is to be yielded is the one that has been crucified with Christ, dead in Christ and death with Christ; buried with Christ and has been made alive with Christ. It is a living body that has been through death and then resurrection. Even the things I bring to Him 100% - without holding anything back, - must be things that have been through death and have come to life through resurrection.

It is for this reason that we cannot just consecrate natural endowments – natural abilities, talents, wisdom, and so on. These being ours from God as Creator and therefore ours in Adam, cannot just be put into new creation work. They must be subjected to death and that to Which God grants resurrection life; only such can be of service in new creation work.

An unbeliever can neither consecrate himself nor consecrate anything that he has to the Lord. An unbeliever and all that he has needs the experience of dying on the cross, being buried, then receiving God's New Life before consecration is possible. So all real service is determined by God, for real service is preceded by resurrection, and only God can grant resurrection life.

The act of yielding

Yielding to God is first of all a major crisis and then a continuous process. This is the same for many spiritual things. Salvation for example is first of all a crises and then a process and then a process and the Spirit-filled life is begum as a crises and then continue as a process. Many of us know the exact moment when we were saved and many of us know the exact moment when, for the first time, the Holy Spirit fell upon us as He fell upon the disciples in the beginning. These are definite, unambiguous experiences. Yielding too must be like that.

God demands that we yield ourselves to Him. We have no choice; we must obey. We are free to postpone it to our loss and detriment but God will never change His mind. A day will never come when He will say,

"Well child, just go on. I will bless you and bring you into all my fullness although you have refused to yield to me."

God has called His children into a life of yieldedness. Those who will obey will be delivered and with Him, overcome. Those who disobey will remain in bondage and overcome. We do well to yield and to do so at once.

Do you know that your old man was crucified with Christ? Have you reckoned yourself dead to sin and alive to God? If you have, you qualify to yield yourself to God. If you are willing, take the decision in your heart and maybe a prayer like the following one expresses that desire.

"Lord Jesus, today the …… day of ……, I……

Give up all my ambitions, plans, desired*s and hopes and I accept Your will for my life. I give you my life, my very being, my all, utterly to be Yours for ever and to be Your only, for ever. I give up my all to be used by You and to be used only by You. I make this surrender to You now in an act of yielding from which nothing in time or eternity will ever release me. I gladly accept Your will for my life, and will continue to accept that will daily whatever it may be. Let me be all that that You saved me for and all that You want me to be, at any cost. I now will that You will and I count on You to continue to will all that You will in all of the future. I want nothing outside of Your perfect will. Lord, posses me and imprison me for You and never allow me one second of liberty away from You nor even the smallest honour or possession outside of Your perfect will? Amen."

After yielding, you must never take back what is yielded. God takes the prayer of yielding seriously and will start to use you on the basis of your declaration in prayer. An ordinary Christian is one thing. A yielded Christian is another thing altogether. My prayer is that all who read this message will on that same day yield themselves without reservation to the Lord Jesus and as such enter into the full deliverance that God offers, and then it will be impossible for sin to reign over them.

Some practical issues for a yielded person

After you have yielded yourself to the Lord Jesus, someone may come to tell you something bad about a brother behind that brother's back. How then do you who yielded yourself to God, to belong exclusively to Him, react to such a move? Normally there would be three possible positions to take:

1. To encourage that brother to speak and to enjoy the gossip.
2. To disapprove of the gossip inwardly but passively listen to it in order not hurt the gossip.
3. To confront the gossip and say to him, *"my ears are holy. They belong exclusively to the Lord Jesus. They must not heart such dirt. Please, do not dirty Jesus' ears."*

The yielded person must act according to the third possibility. He has no choice about it if he is going to continue to live a yielded life.

If someone is invited a yielded person to go and visit some wrong place, the yielded person must tell that one, *"I have no legs."* Why? Because the ones he has belong no more to him but to Jesus. They have no right to go where Jesus will not go. If the yielded person had the legs of his own that did not belong exclusively to Jesus, may be such legs could decide to go with Him, but such legs do not exist, therefore he must not go for that visit.

This also applies to the eyes. They have lost their right to see anything they like. They may see only what Jesus wants them to see. This also applies to the hands of a yielded person. They may touch or handle only the things that Jesus wants them to touch or handled. The property of a yielded person falls into the same way of life. The unyielded person can do with his as he likes. They may give God 10% of it or 20% of it and he uses the rest as he likes. The yielded person has lost his freedom over the property that he is taking care of. He is just a steward. All the property belong to the Lord Jesus. Yes, his salary 100.000 or 400.000francs a month all belong to the Lord Jesus. 10% of it does not belong to Jesus and 90% belongs to him? No! It belong, Jesus 100.000% and He may not use any portion of it without the expressed permission of the rightful owner - the Lord Jesus. This is the way of victory.

It would be impossible for sin to reign in a life that is so yielded to the Lord. The question before us which must be settled before we go on is, *"Are you willing to enter into such life?."* Will you surrender your right to all of your body to the Lord Jesus for all time? Will you break up with all questionable relationships? Will you part with all known sins in your life at all cost? Will you do the above things now? Now?? Now??? Will you do them same for the other issues that will come up in the future which you do not know now?

If you would do it now, you can enter into the full deliverance of God now and as you continue in that way, you will know continued deliverance from the power of sin. If you are hesitant about any of the above issue, do not border to read this book any further. You heart is divided. You are double minded and the Word say to you, *"He who doubts is like a wave of the sea that is driven and tossed by the wind. For that person must not suppose that a double-minded person, unstable in all his ways will receive anything from the Lord"*(James 1:6-8).

THE CRISES

Do you not see where the problem of most believes lies? It is not the fact that they really want to live sanctified lives but cannot. The problem is that for too many, they want to live a *"sanctified"* life but they want to keep some cherished sins or idols. They want to eat their cakes and they want to have their cakes as well.

God cannot do anything for such a person. You must choose now whether you want to be totally freed from the power of sin or not. If you want total freedom, it will have to be from all sins and all sinful relationship as God sees things and this freedom will include the absolute Lordship of the Lord Jesus in all of your life, all that you have and will ever have and for all time.

God must have all in all for total deliverance. You may keep your life in whole or in part for yourself and remain in bondage.

What will you do? If you, like the rich young ruler, turn your back to full deliverance for fear of paying the cost, you will have what you chosen, freedom outside the perfect will of God: life without fullness – Christianity in the continuous or occasional grip of sin and so on, and what use is It ?

We want to add that a person can be carnal an yielded . That is why we insist that knowing and reckoning should precede yielding. A carnal believer is often someone who is baptized in the Holy Spirit but knows very little of the power of the cross to write off his self-life. A carnal believer can have a lot of zeal. Because he has abundant zeal, he thinks along the following lines:

- I must do something for God because I am dead and rises with Christ.
- I must please Christ.
- I must do His will.
- I must do His will now.

- I must do His will quickly, and so on.

He is yielded but he still wants to *"do"*. His *"self"* is still active. Do you see the I, I, I,? The answer is a revelation of the fact that in himself, that is in his flesh, dwells nothing good. When he discovers that, he will yield himself to God and allow the Lord to do the doing.

7

Deliverance from the law

We saw that although the law was given for our good, it did us evil, not because there is something wrong with it, but because there is must that is wrong with us. Before we can enter into our full freedom, we must be delivered from the law or else in yielded state we shall remain in bondage to the law and make no progress. The Bible says,

"Do you not know, brethren, for I am speaking to those who know the law – that the law is binding on a person only during his life? Thus a married woman is bound by law to her husband as long as he lives; but if her husband dies, she is discharged from the law governing the husband. Accordingly, he will be called an adulteress if she lives with another man while her husband is alive. But if her husband dies she is free from that law, and is she marries another man she is not an adulteress.

Likewise my brethren, you have died to the law through the body of Christ, so that you may belong to another, to him who has been raised from the dead in order that we may bear fruit for God. While we were living in the flesh, our sinful passions, aroused by the law, dead to that which held us captive, so that we serve not under the old written code but in the new life of the Spirit" (Romans 7:1-6).

The way of deliverance from the law is by:

Married to another

The believer is not under the law but under grace. The law insists that we do something for God. Grace insists that God has done and is dong something for us. The law says, *"You, do something. You try hard, and so on."* Grace insists that, *"God had done something for you. Be at rest."* As we saw, the demands of the law are righteous. The problem is man. He is a sinner and he is sold – held in bondage in and by sin.

If the demand of the law must be fulfilled and I cannot fulfil them, then someone must fulfil them for me. That is what Jesus did for us. So the picture is painted of a woman married to an exacting man. The man demands that the house should be clean and orderly, the children clean and disciplined and the woman trim and beautiful. The man's demands are not exaggerated. They are just and right and therefore no one would dare ask the man to be less demanding since to do so would be to court disaster. If the woman were the right type – clean, orderly, disciplined and organized, there would be no problem. She would fulfil the man's desires by being herself and would not need to strain. The result would be a healthy and normal marriage.

However, there is a problem. The woman is the problem. She is untidy, disorganized, confused and at home in dirt and disorder. The more she tries to fulfil the man's demands, the more she fails because she cannot be herself and yet be what the man wants her to be. She is therefore in despair. She knows that her husband deserves all that de demands but she finds that she cannot do a thing. She is wretched. Then she sees another man. He is even more demanding than the first man, but he is different. He is willing to stand by her weakness and help her to fulfil near impossible demands. The woman loves this man and would want to marry him and stay with him. The first man is the law. The second man is Christ and the woman is the believer.

The woman cannot marry the second man because she is already married and the marriage bound can only be dissolved by death. If she goes to live with the second man while the first man lives, she would be committing adultery.

There are two ways by which this woman can free herself from the bondage of the first husband and be free to marry the second. The first husband, that is the law, should die, but as we have seen the law cannot die. The Lord Jesus said, *"Think not that I have come to abolish the law and the prophets, I have come not to abolish them but to fulfil them. For truly, I say to you, till heaven and earth pass away, not an iota, not a dot, will pass from the law until all is accomplished. Whosoever them relaxes one of the least of these commandments and teaches men so, shall be called least in the Kingdom of heaven; but h who does them and teaches them shall be called great in the Kingdom of heaven"* (Matthew 5:17-19). Because the law cannot be removed, she must find another way. The second way is that she herself dies and is thereby freed from her husband and then receives life, resurrects and as a new creature is freed to marry the one she loves. This is possible because the Bible says, *"The law is binding on a person only during life."* From the moment that the woman dies, the law that bound her to her first husband is annulled. They are both discharged. If corpses could marry, she as a corps could marry the one she loves, but corpses do not marry. If she is to be married, she must receive life.

We too, were married to the law. The law had its legal demands but we could not fulfil them. The law could not help us to fulfil them; Then the Lord Jesus came along. He loves us and love him. Nevertheless we could not be married to Him because we were already married to the law and a second marriage would have been adultery. So it became necessary for us to die in order to be discharged from the demands of the law. The Lord Jesus helped us to accomplish this. He took us into Himself and when He died, we too died. When He was buried, we too were buried and that brought the legal demands of the law on us and end, for laws do not bind the dead. In dying with Him we were discharged from all our former obligations to the law. The law has lost its claims on us. We are free-delivered from the law.

But we did not only die with Christ. We resurrected with Him. We came to life with Him with a new freedom to be married to the One we love and who loves us, even Jesus Christ our Lord. So we got married to Christ. We are not married to Him. The Bible says, *"Likewise brethren, you have died to the law though the body of Christ, so that you may belong to another, to him who has been raised from the dead in order that we may bear fruit for God. While we were living in the flesh, our sinful passions, aroused by the law, were at work in our members to bear fruit for death. But NOW WE ARE DISCHARGED FROM THE LAW,"* dead to that which held us captive, so that we may serve not under the old written code but in the new life of the spirit" (Romans 7:4-6).

If we have been delivered from the law, then we are free from its demands. There is another way of looking at it. The Lord Jesus said that the law would stand until it was fulfilled. Jesus Christ is our representative fulfilled the law by submitting to its harsh demands by His death on the cross. The Bible says,

"Christ redeemed us from the curse of the law, having become a curse for us – for it is written, 'Cursed be every one who hangs one a tree' " (Galatians 3:13).

Having been delivered from the first husband and his demands and being now married to the new husband, that is Christ, it should be born in mind that this is not an invitation to lawlessness. As we said earlier, the new Husband is more demanding than the laws of the Mosaic code. There is however one big difference. The Lord Jesus is at work in the believer in believer both to will and to do His good pleasure. The believer would find it even it even more impossible to satisfy the demands of Christ on his own but glory be to God, he is not on his own. The Lord is at work is at work in him to ensure that it is possible for him to fulfil the demands of Christ. Remember that all – inclusive death of Christ on the cross has set us free from the law! We are married to another – The Lord Jesus. We bear His name and we share all that He has, including His throne. He fulfils the demands of the law in us (Matthew 5:17); (Philippians 2:13). We are free from doing what the law demands. We simply look up to Jesus and rest in Him and then He does for us and in us what the law could not do.

Sanctification then is experienced in people who are at rest. They have ceased from labouring to satisfy the demands of the law. Those demands are fulfilled in them by Another who dwells in them. Glory be to the Lord!

Do you now see why yielding makes absolute sense? We are to be yielded, not to the old husband (the law) whom we cannot satisfy, but to the new Husband (The Lord Jesus), in whom we delight. Because of this marriage relationship to the Lord Jesus, yielding becomes a delight, for who can resist the One who loves us so completely and who in turn we love without reserve ?

8

The Law of the Spirit of Life in Christ Jesus

We already said that there is law that is operative – the law of sin and death and that it is a very powerful law that cannot be overcome by self-will, determination or any other human effort. I want to also add that it cannot be overcome solely by knowing, reckoning, yielding and being delivered from he law, good as these are.

The law can only be overcome by another law which is stronger that it. That law is more powerful then the law of sin and death is the law of the Spirit of life in Christ Jesus. The Bible says, *"For the law of the Spirit of life in Christ has set me free from the law of sin and death"* (Romans 8:2).

Consider the law of gravity for a moment. It is a very powerful law. It will bring objects down very easily. Although it is a powerful law, it can be overcome. One can be set free from it. Aeroplanes fly and overcome the law for some time. The Lord Jesus, Enoch, and Elijah and many modern spacemen have all gone contrary to the law of gravity. How is this possible?

They must be operating with a force that is stronger than the law of gravity. The law of the Spirit in Christ is stronger than the law of sin and death and because it is stronger, wherever there is a conflict between the two, the law of the Spirit of life in Christ Jesus predominates and wins.

All God's children have been set free from the law of sin and death. My dear brother and sister, you are free. God has done it in Christ!! The Bible says, *"For God has done what the law, weakened by the flesh, could not do: sending his own Son in the likeness of sinful flesh and for sin, he condemned sin in the flesh"* (Romans 8:3).

THE OPERATION OF THE LAW OF THE SPIRIT OF LIFE IN CHRIST

The *"natural walk"* of those who are in the Spirit is spiritual. When a believer has had his eyes also opened to the fact that he has died and is free from the law and therefore married to the Lord Jesus, he must believe by faith that God has put the law of the spirit of life in Christ within him, to operate the victory of God within him against the law of sin and death. If he is ignorant of this, he will not enjoy all the benefits that are his, not because these benefits are not there but because ignorance has robbed him of what is his.

So, the one whose eyes are opened to what is his so that he begins to enjoy them will find that the law of spirit of life in Christ just gains victory for him without strife. Normally, a *"normal"* believer, that is, one who has entered into his inheritance and is enjoying all that is his, will not make an effort to pray, read the Bible, worship or witness. The life in him just flows out effortlessly to the Lord and to others because it flows from the Spirit of Life in him, even the blessed Holy Spirit who life in him.

Before a person is saved or when he is saved but still bound by the law of sin and death, the law of sin and death operates in him so that he sins *"naturally"* and with ease. It all happens in an effortless way. Such a one will have to make a great effort not to sin because not sinning is foreign to his way of life. Take the sin of lying for example. There are people to whom lying is so *"natural"* that it would disturb them if you found fault with them. They are being themselves. If they are not to lie, they must overcome a barrier in order to do so. So occasionally, they exert a force and speak the truth. To such people, Bible study is abnormal, prayer a bore, evangelism near impossible and worship is our of the question. They live in the environment (an inner environment) where the law of sin and death reigns.

When a person is saved and enters into his inheritance by knowing, reckoning, yielding and accepting God's facts of his deliverance from the law and marriage to Christ, an addition to the fact that God's mighty victory law – the law of the Spirit in Christ has been put into him to enable him to life a holy life, the law of the Spirit of life in Christ Jesus will become operative in him and he will have to make an effort to sin. He will have to make an effort not to witness. For example, he will have to make an effort by building all excesses against the inner promptings of the Holy Spirit that tell him to let the life of Christ flow out in witness to the unbeliever. Each time, he sins, he will have to overcome a big barrier before he does anything that God does not want and he would feel pain inside him as he overcomes the barrier and disobeys or make a special effort and harden his conscience in order to reduce the pain that sin causes him.

Therefore, it is spiritually normal that Christ produces the righteous demands of the law in us. The Bible says, *"For God has done what the law, weakened by flesh, could not do: sending his own Son in the likeness of sinful flesh and sin, he condemned sin in the flesh, in order that the just requirements of the law might be fulfilled in us who walk not according to the flesh but according to the Spirit"* (Romans 8:3-4). Christ does this by the law of the spirit of life in Christ Jesus. At the basis of the law is the Lord Jesus who by His death on the cross, His resurrection and His enthronement guarantees that *"The law of the Spirit of life in Christ Jesus"* will always work in those who walk after the Spirit.

My beloved brethren, I want to assure you that this law is at work in you. Do you remember the things that you used to love so dearly? Do you also remember the things that you used to love so dearly? Do you always remember that without any effort on your part the love for them went away completely? Can you not look at your character and see that it has changed and that the change has been radical and far-reaching? The change took place so gradually and unconsciously that you did not know that it was taking place. Do you now find that you love people that you did not and could not before? Have you not found that some people you once taught were very terrible now appear to you as wonderful? All these changes are because of a law at work in you. You are obeying it often without noticing it and the result of that continuous obedience is the changes we have been talking about.

The limits of the law of the spirit of life in Christ

The law of the Spirit of life in Christ Jesus does not just operate in a haphazard way. It operates within certain boundaries. No one should therefore go ahead and say, *"Because the law of spirit of life is at work in me, I can go anywhere and do anything and it will always work."* Even laws have their limitations. Take the law of gravity for example. It operates within the limits of the earth's gravitational pull. Outside that, it is non-operative. The law of the spirit of life in Christ Jesus sets us free from the law of sin and death into its own share of operation.

Outside its sphere of operation, too, is powerless. The question then arises, *"What is that sphere of operation of the law of the spirit of life in Christ Jesus? Where can I as a believer move and be sure that I am covered by that law and it will therefore not be overcome bye the law sin and death?"*

To answer this question, we musty look at that law itself. It is the law of the spirit of life in Christ.

The spirit of life is none but the blessed Holy Spirit. So, it is the law of the Holy Spirit operative in the Lord Jesus or operative as it operates in the Lord Jesus. We therefore say that the law of the spirit of life in Christ Jesus is the law of the Holy Spirit operative in the yielded believer as it operated in the Lord Jesus.

So, for that law to be fully operative, for us to know its full protection, we must be where Jesus wants us to be, when He wants us to be there, doing what He wants us to do.

So the law only fully covers those who are in the centre of God's will. In the centre of God's will the law of sin and death is totally important and the law of the spirit of life in Christ Jesus fully operative.

This requires two basic things. First of all, it requires that the believer should know the mind of God about everything he is to do. He cannot just go anywhere, any time or do just anything. This will be to cause disaster. Secondly, it requires that the believer should do God's will. What he knows, he must put into practice. Is this not the reason for which the Holy Spirit was given? Was he not given so that He would lead God's children into a knowledge of God's will and that He would give then the power to do it? He who was given for this purpose dwells in us and has a law to operate within us. Let us give Him the opportunity to do His work.

The limits of the law of the Spirit of life in Christ Jesus is the full presence of the Lord Jesus.

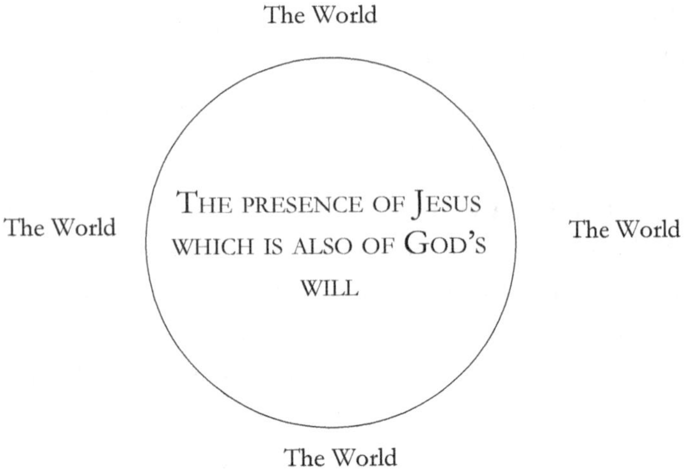

Ce cercle représente la présence de Jésus-Christ qui est aussi le centre de la volonté de Dieu. Il représente aussi les limites de la loi de l'Esprit de vie en Jésus-Christ. À l'intérieur de ce cercle, un croyant marche dans la pureté, car la loi du péché et de la mort y est impuissante. Loin du cercle, c'est le monde et la loi du péché et de la mort y règne.

This circle represents the presence of Jesus which is also which is also the centre of God's will. It also represents the limits of the law of the Spirit of life in Christ Jesus. Within that circle a believer walks in purity, for the law of sin and death are important there. Away from that circle is the world and the law of sin and death reigns there.

If a believer strays away from the presence of Jesus (the centre of God's will) either deliberately or through ignorance, he loss the protective enough. If a believer sincerely but mistakenly walks away from God's will, he will not be prevented by his sincerity from sinning. The only protection is in the presence of Jesus, in the centre of God's will.

HIS LAWS OF THE HEARTS

How can a believer determine the limit beyond which the law of the Spirit of life in the Lord Jesus does not operate and where he will therefore face the law of sin and death and succumb to it? I want to say that the yielded believer will know. This is possible because the limits will be determined by the Holy Spirit within him. He will operate the law of the Spirit of life in the Lord Jesus not only to set free from the law of sin and death but also to guide. He will put a new law in the heart of the believer and that new law; the law of the Spirit of life in Christ Jesus governed by the Holy Spirit, will enable the believer to know in his inner man that he must:do this, not do this, say this, not say this, go here or not go here.

The yielded believer will know how far he can go, where he can go, when he can go and with whom he can go. He will also know where he may not go, and so on. The law is written on his heart. The Lord had promised that the day would come when the law would be ion the heart. When a person truly believes in the Lord, that day begins for him. The Lord promised saying: "Behold, the days are coming, says the Lord, when I will make a new covenant with he house of Israel and with the house of Judah. It will not be like the covenant which I made with their forefathers when I took them by the hand to bring them out of Egypt, my covenant which I will make with the house of Israel after those days, says the Lord. I will put my law within them, and I will write it upon their hearts; and I will be their God, and they shall be my people. And no longer shall each man teach his brother, saying, *'Know the Lord'* for they shall all know me, from the least of them to the greatest, says the Lord; or I for they shall all know me, from the least of them to the greatest, says the Lord; or I 34).

So God decided that the final way of having things put right was to put the law not on stones; not on sheets of papers but on the heart. The prophets continued to prophesy that this would happen. The prophet Ezekiel, speaking as the mouthpiece of God, said:

"I will sprinkle clean water upon you, and you shall be clean from all your uncleannesses, and from all your idols, I will clean you. A new heart I will give you, and a new spirit I will put within you; and I will take out of your flesh the heart of stone and give you a heart of flesh. I will put my spirit within you, and cause you to walk in my statues and be careful to observe my ordinances" (Ezekiel 36:25-27).

The apostle Paul writes about this new covenant in the following way, *"Our competence is from God, who has made us competent to be ministers of a new covenant, not in a written code but in the Spirit; for the written code kills but the Spirit gives life"* (2 Corinthians 3:5-6).

9

Walking in the Spirit

The bible says that, God's purpose is that the just requirements of the law should not be run away from but that they should

"Be fulfilled in us, who walk not according to the flesh but according to the Spirit" (Romans 8:4).

This makes walking by the Spirit a *'must'* for all who want to go far with the Lord. The question then arises, *"What does it mean to walk by the Spirit?"* It means to allow the Holy Spirit to do that which the law, the flesh, self and the rest do.

When a person of surrendered, he is not called to sit passively and do nothing. Such a one will become and easy prey of the wicked one. From the moment of surrender to the Lord Jesus, he must start to walk as the Holy Spirit leads and so obey the commands of Christ, being enabled to do so by the Holy Spirit. This walk is most easy. It is the only easy walk in the spiritual realm. For example, the Lord Jesus would say, *"Son, do this for me. I provide the power of my Holy Spirit, resident in you, to enable you to do it."* An the believer would say, *"Yes my Lord."* I am willing to do it. I will go at once and do it and accept the power of resident Holy Spirit for its accomplishment. Nevertheless

Lord, I do not want to do it alone. Come and do it with me. Come and do it through me." Can the Lord fail to respond to such a prayer? No! Never!!

So, this way of walking makes even the weakest saint powerful. He is a co-labourer with Christ. When he is weak, the Lord in him is strong and the Lord's strength is made perfect fir him I his weaknesses, so that he too like the great apostle can say, *"I will all the more gladly boast of my weaknesses, that the power of Christ man rest upon me. For the sake of Christ then, I am content with weaknesses, insults, hardships, persecutions, and calamities, for when I am weak, then I m strong"* (2 Corinthians 12:9-10).

In this walk there is constant victory even as Jesus is Victor. Jesus is the beginning of that walk and because He has been made our sanctification, the walk is sanctified and those who thus walk are sanctified. He is the Sustainer of the walk and that means that the walk is sustained in holiness and sanctification. Yes, the Lord is at the centre of the walk, making His sanctified life to be felt and experienced in the one in whom He is working to make the walk possible. Jesus is also the end of this walk. As the end, He brings all who would have walked with Him to entire sanctification and redemption. The Bible says, *"He is the source of your life in Christ Jesus, whom God made our wisdom, our righteousness and sanctification and redemption"* (1 Corinthians 1:30). *"May the God of peace himself sanctify you wholly; and may your spirit and soul and body be kept sound and blameless at the coming of our Lord Jesus Christ. He who calls you is faithful, and he will do it"* (1 Thessalonians 5:23-24). Because he is the end, He will bring our sanctification to the end: to a completion. He has started it. He will not fail to accomplish it.

Walking by the Spirit is to give everything to Jesus and to follow Him in everything. It is the way of

immediate obedience,

glad obedience,

complete obedience,

continuous obedience and

costly obedience.

Walking by the Spirit the way of the gospel, for the gaol of the gospel is to give everything to God. Total obedience now and always ensures that that aim of the gospel is accomplished, that is, it ensures that everything is given back to the Lord.

Following Him in everything means yielding to Him in everything. As we have said before, it begins with a crisis but it continuous day by day in an increasing measure as even the smallest demands of the Lord are obeyed.

Walking by the Spirit puts an end to the desires of the flesh. Many of God's children focus their eyes on the desires and activities of the flesh in them and keep wondering how they can put these desires to an end and then they gaze at the desires of the flesh, the more they will find themselves desiring what they very much want to run away from and soon they find that they are trapped.

The apostle Paul says, *"Walk by the Spirit and do not gratify the desires of the flesh"* (Galatians 5:16).As the believer walks in the Spirit, the walk in Spirit will so absorb him that there will be no room for the desires of the flesh. In a sense, the answer to the flesh is a total pre-occupation with the desires of the Holy Spirit.

This walk is not passive but active. It is involving and co-operation with Christ who, by the Holy Spirit, does the walking in us. In full assurance that this is possible and normal, the apostle commands, *"There, putting away falsehood, let everyone speak the truth with his neighbour, for we are members one to another. Be angry but do not sin, do not let the sun go down on your anger and give opportunity to the devil. Let the thief no longer steal, but rather let him labour, doing hones work with his hands, so that he may be able to give to those in need. Let no evil talk come out of your mouths, but only such as is good for edifying, as fits the occasion, that it may impart grace to those who hear. And do not grieve the Holy Spirit of God, in whom you are sealed for the day of redemption. Let all bitterness and with and anger and clamour and slander be put away from you, with all malice, and be kind to one another, tender-hearted, forgiving one another, as God in Christ forgave you"* (Ephesians 4:25-32).

Is this possible? Yes, very possible with Christ and therefore very possible in us because these are the righteous requirements of the law and they are fulfilled in us by Him. For God is at work in us (By Christ Jesus through the power of His Holy Spirit) both to will and to do is good pleasure, (Philippians 2:12). We can do all things through Christ who strengthens us (Philippians 4:13).

The believer's life – the supernatural life

God has called us not the natural life of the sons of men but to the supernatural life of the sons of God. This life would be impossible outside of Christ. He has called us to commandments that are so far above commandments that He gave to Moses. Look at these, *"You have heard that it was said,* "An eye and a tooth for a tooth." *But I say to you,* "Do not resist one who is evil. But if anyone strikes you a the right cheek, turn to him the other also, and if any one would sue you and take your coat, let him have your cloak as well, and if any one forces you go one mile, go with him two miles. Give to him he begs from you, and do not refuse him who would borrow from you" (Matthew 5:38-42).

1. Rejoice and be exceedingly glad when persecuted. "You have heard that it was said of the men of old, *'You shall not kill; and whoever kills shall be liable to judgment. 'But I say to you that everyone who is angry with his brother shall be liable to judgment; whoever insults his brother shall be liable to the council, and whoever says, 'You fool!'* shall be liable to hell of fire. So if you are offering your gift at the altar and there remember that your brother has something against you, leave your gift there before the altar and go, first be something against you, leave your gift there before the altar and go, first be 25).

a. So, if you are angry with your brother you are liable to judgment. b) If you say, *'You fool!'* you shall be liable to the hell of fire.

b. Gifts unto God without reconciliation at the human level re rejected by God.

2. *"You have heard that it was said, 'You shall not commit adultery.' But I say to you that every one who looks at a woman lustfully has already committed adultery with her in his heart. If your right eye causes you to sin, pluck it out and throw it away, it is better that you lose one of your members than that your whole body be thrown into hell. And if your right hand caused you to sin, cut it off*

and throw it away; it is better that you lose one of your members than that your whole body go into hell" (Matthew 5:27-30).

a. So, immoral thoughts are as serious as immoral actions before God. b) It is better to lose any part of the body and go to heaven than have a complete body and be lost in hell.

3. *"You have heard that it was said, 'You shall not love your neighbour and have your enemy.' But I say to you, 'Love your enemies and pray for those who persecute you, so that you may be sons of your Father who is in heaven, for he makes his sun rise on the evil and on the good and sends rain on the just and sun the unjust. For if you love those who love you what reward have you? Do not even the tax collectors do the same? And if you salute only your brethren, what more are you doing than others? DO not even the Gentiles do the same? You, therefore, must be perfect as your heavenly Father is perfect"* (Matthew). *"Thus, when you give alms, sound no trumpet before you, as the hypocrites do in the synagogues and in the streets, so that they be praised by men. Truly, I say to you, they have received their reward. But when you give alms do not let your let hand know what your right hand is doing, so that your alms may be in secret; and your Father who sees in secret will reward you"* (Matthew 6:2-4). So, deed done with the purpose of receiving praise from men receive no reward from the heavenly Father. He rewards that which is done with the purpose of satisfying Him and Him alone.

4. *"Do not lay up for yourselves treasures on earth, where moth and rust consume and where thieves break in and steal, but lay up for yourselves treasures I heaven where neither moth nor rush consumes and where thieves do not break in and steal. For where your treasure is, there will your heart be also"* (Matthew 6:19-21). So, lay up no treasures on earth for they will make you earthly-minded.

5. *"No one can serve two masters. For either he will hate one and love the other, or he will be devoted to the one and despise the other. You cannot serve God and Mammon"* (Matthew 6:24). So, only those who set hearts on worldly riches despise and hate God.

6. *"Enter by the narrow gate; for the gate is wide and the way is easy that leads to destruction, and those who enter by it are many. For the gate is narrow and hard, that leads to life and those who fine it are few"* (Matthew 7:13-14). So only those who are prepared to enter by the narrow gate will be saved.

7. *"Beware of false prophets, who come to you in sheep's clothing but inwardly are ravenous wolves. You will know them by their fruits. Are grapes gathered from thorns, or figs from thistles? So every sound tree bears good fruit, but bad tree bears evil fruit. A sound tree cannot bear evil fruit, nor can a bad tree bear good fruit. Every tree that does not bear good fruit is cut down and thrown into the lake of fire. Thus you will know them by their fruits"* (Matthew 7:15-20). So the content of a man's character is more important than his speech. And uselessness invites disaster.

8. *"Not everyone who says to me, Lord, Lord shall enter the kingdom of heaven, but he who does the will of my Father who is in heaven. One that day many will say to me, 'Lord, did we not prophesy in your name, and cast out demons in your name, and do many mighty works in your name?' And then will I declare to them,* "I never knew you; depart from me, you evil doers" (Matthew 7:21-23). So the Lord wants holiness without which even miracles are useless.

So we see something of the demands of the Lord Jesus. At the human level these demands are impossible. To the worldly-minded, they are stupid and foolish. But the believer is not human. He is superhuman! The supernatural Christ has taken us to His death on the cross, to His burial in the tomb, to His resurrection and to His enthronement. We too have been rendered superhuman, supernatural in Him. That is why we can do these supernatural things that would otherwise be impossible. Can you imagine loving an enemy without Christ or not laying up any treasures on earth without him? This would be both undesirable and impossible. Yet these things flow out of God's supernatural people – the believers. Christ has worked out His character in them so such an extent that they are sometimes surprised by the extent of the change. Glory be to God! To be led in this kind of life is the lot of all the children of God who are prepared to let the Lord work in them (Romans 8:15). And as they are thus led, the Holy Spirit witnesses with their spirits that they are the children of God (Romans 8:16).

How can we thank God enough for doing this in us and for us? How can we glorify Him and His Christ? I feel that the words of the twenty-four elders come slightly close to what I would love us to say to Him. Let us use their words to praise Him and after using their words; let us use our own:

"Worthy are thou, our Lord and God, to receive glory and honour and power, for thou didst create all things, and by thy will they existed and were created" (Revelation 4:11). *"Worthy are thou to take the scroll and to open its seals, for thou waste slain and by thy blood didst ransom men for God from every tribe and tongue and people and nation, and hast made them a kingdom and priest to our God, and they shall reign on earth"* (Revelation 5: 9-10).

10

The Mind and the Walk in the Spirit

The mind plays an important role in the walk by the Spirit. A man is what he thinks and not what he is. A man's thoughts betray who he is and also make him into what he will be.

The Bible says, *"If then you have raised with Christ, seek the things that are above, where Christ is seated at the right hand of God. Set your minds on things that are above, not on things that are on earth. For you have died, and your life is hid with Christ in God. When Christ who is our life appears, then you will also appear with Him in glory. Put to death therefore what is earthly in you: fornication, passion, evil desire, and covetousness, which is idolatry. On account of these, the wrath of God is coming. In these you once walked when you lived in them. But now put all away: anger, wrath, malice, slander, and foul talk from your mouth. DO not lie to one another, seeing that you have put off the old nature which practices and have put on the new nature, which is being renewed in knowledge after the image of its creator. Here there cannot be Greek and Jew, circumcised and uncircumcised, Barbarian, Scythian, slave, free man, but Christ is all and in all. Put on then, as God's chosen ones, holy and beloved, compassion, kindness, lowliness, meekness, and patience, forbearing and one another and, if one has a complaint against another, forgiving each other; as the Lord has forgiven you, so you must forgive. Above all these, put on love, which binds everything together in perfect harmony. And let the peace of Christ rule in your hearts, to which indeed you were called in the body. And be thankful. Let the word of God dwell in you richly; teach and admonish one another in all wisdom, and sins psalms and hymns and spiritual songs with thanksgiving in your hearts to God. And whatever you do, in word or deed, do everything in the name of the Lord Jesus, giving thanks to God the father through him"* (Colossians 3:1-17).

"For those who live according to the flesh set their minds in the things of the flesh, but those who live according to the spirit set their minds on the things of the spirit. To set the mind on the flesh is death, but to set the mind on the spirit is life and peace. For the mind that is set on the flesh is hostile to God; it does not submit to Gods law, indeed it cannot; and those who are in the flesh cannot please God. But you are not in the flesh, you are in the spirit, if in fact the spirit of God dwells in you. And anyone who does not have the spirit of Christ odes not belong to Him. But if Christ is in you, although your bodies are dead because of sin, your spirits are alive because of righteousness. If the spirit of Him who raised Jesus from the dead dwells in you, he who raised Christ Jesus from the dead will give life to your mortal bodies also through his Spirit which dwells in you. So, then, brethren, we are debtors, not to the flesh, to live according to he flesh – for if you live according to the flesh, you will die, but if by the Spirit you put to death the deeds of the body, you will live" (Romans 8:5-13).

We said that walking in the Spirit is not passive but active. Involves:

1. Seeking the things that are above.
2. Setting the mind on things that are above.
3. Putting the death what is earthly in you.
4. Putting off the old nature.
5. Putting on the new nature.

6. Allowing the peace of Christ to rule.
7. Allowing the Word of Christ to dwell in you richly.
8. Teaching and admonishing in all wisdom.
9. Singing Psalms, songs and so on.
10. Singing the mind on the things of the spirit.
11. Being debtors to the Spirit.

It means that a believer could also decide to:

1. Seek the things that are below.
2. Set the mind on things that are below.
3. Allow what is earthly in him to live and grow.
4. Allow the old nature to remain.
5. Refuse to put on the new nature.
6. Refuse to allow the peace of Christ to rule.
7. Refuse to allow the Word of Christ to dwell richly in him.
8. Refuse to teach or be taught and be admonished in all wisdom.
9. Refuse to sing Psalms, songs with thankfulness in his heart to God.
10. Set his mind on the things of the flesh.
11. Become a debtor to the flesh.

So there is a choice to make and to make and to a great extent the believer is what he chooses. What a person thinks decides what he becomes. We become the sum total of our thoughts and choices. The believer's mind matters. The mind has an important part to play in our deliverance and walk in the Spirit. The Bible says that the believer should set his mind on things that are above; and to set the mind on the things of the Spirit.

The question that arises is, *"Which mind is to be the things of the Spirit?"* This is important because a human being can have one of the following types of minds:

1. The unregenerate (blinded) mind.
2. The regenerate but double mind.
3. The regenerate and renewed mind.

We shall look at these three minds in some detail. I want to acknowledge that most of the material here is not mine. It is material first given to brother Marshall of Australia by the Lord.

The mind is the communication centre for the whole man. It receives a whole mass of information inputs, impressions and messages from different sources, and continues sorts, analyses, evaluates and appraises these inputs. Many, probably the vast majority, are stored away for future reference, but the selected ones are presented to the will for adoration. Those that are sealed ultimately affect our behaviour. The mind receives information from six main sources.

1. The world

The mind receives information about the external environment: the weather, the people around, and so on. This information is morally neutral. It does not draw to or away from God. But the information is also received from the spiritual world. The spiritual world is comprised of the whole condition of human affairs, in a state of alienation from God and in opposition to Him. So everyday, the mind is flooded with its culture, its values, its judgment, its opinions and its propaganda. The apostle John wrote, *"We know that we are of God, and the whole world is in the power of the evil one"* (1 John 5:19). So through the radio, television, the printed page, the world presses itself on the mind of everyone.

2. The flesh

The flesh is the world within – the internal environment. The flesh is the sum of all the desires, appetites, needs and drives of man in his alienation and hostility to God. The flesh figures prominently in temptations. The Bible says, *"Let no one say when tempted,* "I am tempted by God; for God cannot with evil and he himself tempts on one, but each person is tempted when he is lured en enticed by his own desires. Then desire, when it has conceived, gives birth to sin; and sin when it is full – grown brings forth death" (James 1: 13-15).

3. The devil

The devil has access to the mind of man, even to the mind of the believer. The apostle Paul wrote to the Corinthians, *"But I am afraid that as the serpent deceived Eve by his cunning, your thoughts (mind) will be led astray from a sincere and pure devotion to Christ"* (2 Corinthians 11:3).

The devil uses this access to plant temptations in the mind. Sometimes even believers who are mature have wicked thoughts suddenly coming, as if from no where, into their minds. These thoughts come not from inside but from the wicked one. No one is responsible for such thoughts. Their presence in the mind does not constitute sin. If they are rejected at once, no sin is committed. If they are harboured, they lead to sin and the one who harbours them is responsible for them and reaps what they produce. There is threefold Satanic attack on the mind:

1. By Suggestion: When the Lord Jesus spoke to the disciples about the cross, Peter took Him aside and began to rebuke him. *"But turning and seeing his disciples, He rebuked Peter, and said,* "Get behind me, Satan! For you are not on the side of God, but of me" *Satan was there suggesting,* "Do not go to the cross."

2. By interference: The devil seeks to takes God's Word out of a man's mind. In the parable of the sower, the Bible says about the seed that fell along the path, *"And these are the ones along the path, where the world is sown, when they hear, Satan immediately comes and takes away the word that is sown in them"* (Mark 4:15).

3. By domination: This is the ultimate goal of the devil – to fill, to dominate, to take complete control. The Bible, in talking of Ananias, said that the devil had filled his heart to lie to the Holy Ghost and to keep back part of the proceeds of the land (Acts 5:3).

4. The human spirit

Even though man is dead in trespasses and sins, the spirit of the unregenerate man is still existing. Man still has a spirit. The Spirit of man is dead in that it is separated from God (and that is what the Bible calls death) and not because it is non-existent.

Man's spirit though dead is still capable of contacting the spirit world. Because man's spirit is in a state of death, it can only contact those spirit beings who are in a state of death, that is, evil spirit. That is why unregenerate man can have a spiritual experience but not with the Holy Spirit.

The messages that come into the mind from the spirit of a man are in three main forms:

1. **The voice of conscience** : Conscience is not the voice of God and it is not infallible. The conscience can be defiled. Conscience is not a rational faculty. You cannot reason with conscience. It passes categorical judgment on behaviours and says, *"This is right"* or *"This is wrong"*. You can give your conscience many reasons for doing a thing but conscience will still say that it is wrong. The human conscience has a form and a content. In form, conscience is universal. It operates exactly the same way I every human being regardless of race, sex, culture, etc. It passes categorical judgment on behaviour. In content, this is, the basis on which conscience makes its categorical judgments vary so that one man's conscience may condemn him for something about which another person's conscience is neutral or even approves. The judgments conscience make are through upbringing and learning in family and society have been internalized or as the Bible puts it, written on their heart (Romans 2:15). Man's conscience can be defiled and when defiled, it can from that defiled standard give depraved and perverse judgements that are contrary to the law of God.

2. **Intuition** : This is the immediate perception that comes directly to us, without any intermediate mental steps. It is not the result of rational, deductive mental process. Human intuition is not infallible but it is spiritual; it is the human

spirit receiving knowledge. Because of sin and the fact that man is finite, man perceives knowledge imperfectly and often misinterprets what is received. What is received intuitively is passed on to the mind.

3. **Communion** : This is the same as communication. Even at the human level, we do not communicate unless we reach out in our spirit to another. Without that, we are only exchanging words. The only way we communicate with God is by reaching out to Him with our spirit. *"God is spirit and those who worship him must worship him in spirit and truth"* (John 4:24).

5. The voice of God

Although man has sinned and rebelled, he is still within the reach of God. God still speak to the unregenerate man. He spoke to Adam and Eve after the sinned. He spoke to Moses in the burning bush. God still speaks to people.

6. The past

The mind also receives messages from the past in the form of memory. So people recall memories of the past, of

- joy
- triumph,
- success,
- failure,
- hurt,
- disappointment,

- dreams that have never been fulfilled,
- and the rest

All these are offered to the mind.

These six sources make offers to man's mind. What dominates the mind dominates man. Knowing this, we shall look at the three different minds are possible and then we see why a renewed mind is part of the secret of sanctification :

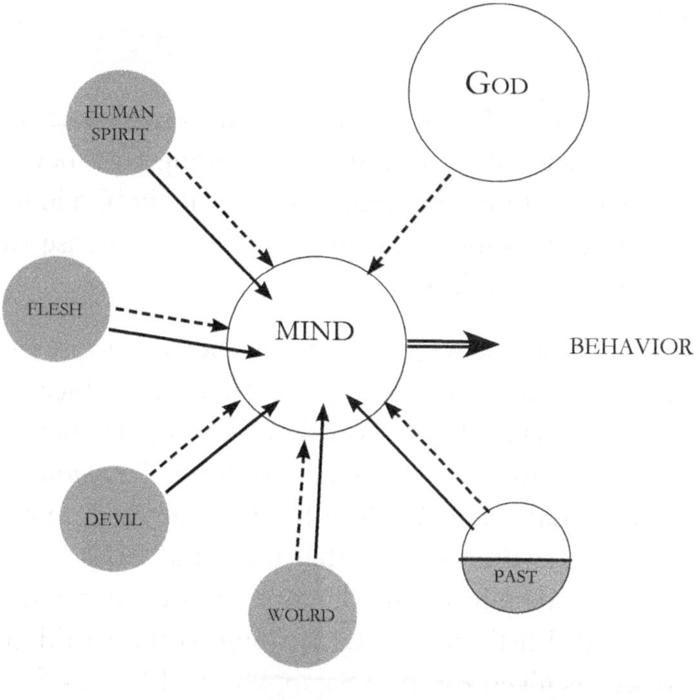

The unregenerated (blinded) mind

- - - -➤ This indicate communication (i.e) suggestions. It is the offer of information that at the disposal of the mind whether to accept or reject

⟶ This indicate lines of authority. The suggestions are made but not left to discretion of the mind. These is insistence that they are adopted

How is authority established?

Authority is established by obedience. Whatever we habitually obey thereby possesses a blinded authority over our minds. If the Word is to have authority over our lives, we must obey it. If we want the Holy Spirit to have authority over our live, there is only one way to it – we must obey Him. If the impulses of

- fear
- doubt,
- resentment

and so on are obeyed, they will have authority over our minds. The problem of man is that by yielding to (obeying) temptation, he has allowed temptations to create in him in him and in his sources binding authority so that they exercise rule and dominion over his mind.

Through man's disobedience, the world has become more than an external temptation. Its values, standards and objectives have become internalized. The world rules in man's mind so that men, whether they like it or not, become *"conformed to the world."* In the same way the flesh has been given dominion over dominion over the mind so that the mind is set on the flesh, thus man finds himself fulfilling the desires of the flesh and of the mind. Furthermore, by yielding to the world and the flesh, man has given room to Satan who is the god of this world to have authority over our the mind. The apostle said, *"And their case the god of this world has blinded the minds of flesh unbelievers to keep them from seeing the light of the gospel of Christ, who is the likeness of God"* (2 Corinthians 4:3-4).

In other word, Satan uses the authority man has given him to shut up the human mind against God.

In thinking about the whole matter of obedience and authority, I find that it permeates every area of life. The person who yields to a temptation for the first time normally frights a lot before he succumbs, but with increasing times of yielding, it becomes increasingly easy until all the barriers seem broken and there is a restraint. The person who says *"no"* to hunger can continue to go without food for long. However, the person who eats each time the slightest desire for food comes will develop in that direction until he needs, five meals a day. During a fast, here sill be the initial hunger pangs. If *"no"* is them, they will go away for some time. After some time they will come again. If they encounter another *"no"* they will further withdraw. If on the other hand they are welcome the first time, then they will come again with greater insistence.

Repentance is a change of mind. When a person repents and believes in the Lord Jesus, he is born from above by the power of the Holy Spirit. In the recreated spirit of the believer, the Holy Spirit now dwells. As he illumines the human spirit, the conscience now begins to deal with the mind. It becomes sensitive to sin and obedience. As he obeys, the Holy Spirit gains authority in the mind, opening it to understand the Scriptures. The mind is now enlightened (regenerated).

THE ENLIGHTENED BUT DOUBLE MIND

Sometimes a very strong experience of grace at conversion has a power effect in ridding the mind of the dominion and authoritative power to sinful habits. But this is not always the case. Like Lazarus after he came out of the grave, many remain bound by grave-clothes.

Furthermore, the world, the flesh, and the devil are constantly striving to regain ground that has been lost. If the devil, the flesh ort he world are obeyed, he person gets back to the same bondages in the mind. Bondage may also come through a failure to walk in victory. The state of the mind is as illustrated. Some areas are full of light and open to the Lord, others are dominated by darkness. Between the two, the dividing line is a kind of moving frontier that reflects the vitality or otherwise of the experience at the moment. There is a way in the mind. In this condition, although the mind is open to the revelation of the divine truth and the prompting of the Holy Spirit, it is open to other things as well. Old thoughts patterns or temptations become persistent and wear the person down into defeat and despair. The trouble is that areas of the mind are still under the control of the old masters. Into these areas that are under their control, they inject their poison. Some of their works are as follows:

The flesh pours out the poison described in Galatians 5:19-21. These include impure and sensual thoughts, jealousy, animosity, bad temper, outbursts of anger, selfishness, malice, envy and hate.

The world will produce jealousy, selfish ambitions (James 3:14-15), worry (Mark 4:19), deception and doubt (1 John 4:1-3).

Satan has a mark in all these but the particular marks of his personal attacks include fear (Hebrews 2:14), depression (darkness) (Ephesians 6:12), resentment and unforgiving spirit (2 Corinthians 2:10) and pride (1 Timothy 3:6).

The past – the hard, harsh and sarcastic things said in childhood can remain most destructive. Hurt feelings may become the ruling force of a life that seeks revenge in one way or the other. Guilt and condemnation for the pact can steal peace and assurance from a being to a far – reaching extent.

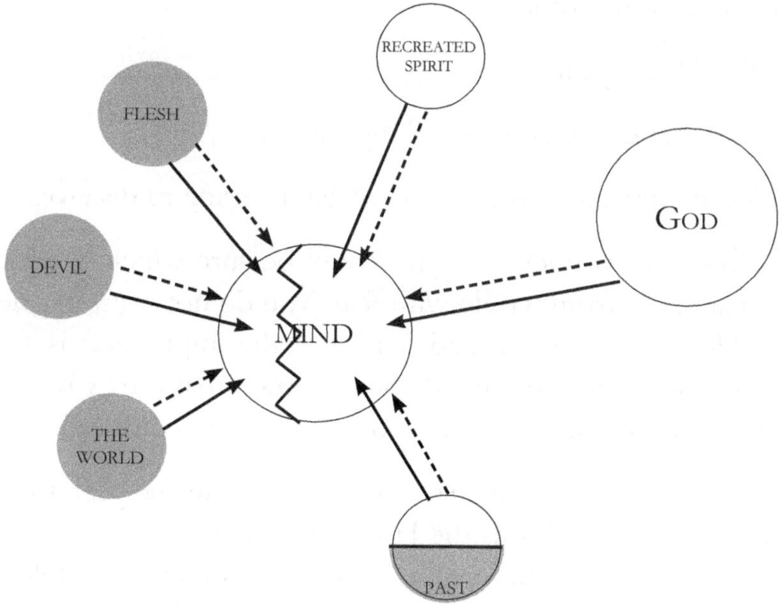

The Enlightened but double mind

Lines of suggestions

Lignes of autority

Do you see the mind we have just described as yours? There are certainly times of blessing when light flooded in and darkness was out. There are spiritually low moments when the light is almost put out by the uprising of the old problems. Your mind is double and unstable as the Bible puts it in James.

In this state of mind there is a real problem with guidance. You have an impression in your mind but you do not know whether or not it came from:

1. The Holy Spirit,

2. Personal fleshy desires seeking fulfilment,

3. Satan (appearing as an angel of light) trying to deceive.

Do you not wonder how you could be sure which is which? You are torn from within with fear. You do not want to grieve the Holy Spirit by not acting in case the impression is from Him and on the other hand you are afraid that it may be from your flesh or from the wicked one and you re confused.

I was once involved in such a mess. It was in the year 1970. I had been baptized into the Holy Spirit that same year, in fact just a few months before the incident I am about to tell you of. I thought that all the voices that came to me I n prayer would be from the Lord. I loved the Lord in an intense way since I was baptized into the Holy Spirit and my being was set on fire for Him. One night, a brother whom I shall call *"L"* and I were deep in prayer. Then I heard a voice talking to me. It said, *"I am the Lord. I want to talk to you."* We stopped praying and brother *"L"* took a pen and paper and began to record what came forth. We were to go to a brother, *"M"* , who was a cripple, at 5 p.m. the next day and tell him, *"In the name of Jesus, walk."* He would walk immediately. We spent the rest of the night rejoicing. We could hardly wait until 5 p.m. the next day. We met at 4p.m., prayed, and moved to brother *"M's"* room. The instructions we received had told us that we would find him in his room but at five o'clock. When we got there, he wasn't there. He came at 5:30 p.m. and we started.

We gave the formula word of command that we had received and nothing happened. We went and held his leg and cried and cried to God like the prophets of Baal on Mount Camel and nothing happened. After three hour' labour, we stopped, defeated, and frustrated. We had listened to the enemy and had been deceived.

More could be said about the double mind, but have you not been shocked by the conduct of believers? Have you never been shocked your own actions to the extent that you wonder how a child of God could think, say and do some of the things you have said, thought, and done?

A believer can commit all the sins listed in the Bible if he allows the old master to rule. He can even commit sins that he did not commit as an unbeliever. It is not the committing nor the non committing of some acts of the flesh that makes him a child of God.

A renewed mind is possible. The Bible says, *"Do not be conformed to this world but be transformed by the renewal of your mind, that you may prove what is the will of God, what is good and acceptable and perfect"* (Romans 12:2-3). So from this passage the following come out clearly:

The way not to conform to the world is not by struggling not to conform to this or that, that is of the world, but by the renewing of the mind. The renewed mind is the answer to the temptation to conform to the world. Also, the way to discover and to prove God's good, acceptable and perfect will is through a renewed mind.

The Word of God further commands, *"Put off your old nature which belongs to your former manner of life and is corrupt through deceitful lust, and be renewed in the spirit of your minds, and put on the new nature created after the likeness of God in true righteousness and Holiness"* (Ephesians 4 :22-23). Here then is God's way to freedom. It is not the two stages of putting off and putting on but in three stages:

1. Put off the old nature,

2. Be renewed in the spirit of your mind.

3. Put on the new self.

Could that be the source of the problem with many saints? They have *"putt off"* alright but they *"put on"* the regenerate but double mind landed on the same problem as before. The way of success is through the renewed mind.

The renewed mind : how acquired

1. Recognise the work on the cross:

The Lord Jesus said of the devil, *"The ruler of the world comes and has nothing in me"* (John 14: 13). In the man Jesus, there was absolutely nothing that could give Satan any authority over Him at all – no sin, no failure, and no yielding. Then at the cross, the humanity of Jesus became a corporate humanity that embraced all who would believe on Him, for He said, *"Now is the judgment of this world, now shall the ruler of this world be cast out; and I, when I am lifted up from the earth, will draw all men to myself"* (John 12:31-32). On the cross, the Lord Jesus incorporated all believers into Himself and yielded Himself to the powers of darkness (Luke 22:53) and by His death and resurrection shattered forever those powers. Because we were taken into His humanity, we too died with Him, we too have been raised with Him and we too have been exalted. So the cross answered:

- The world (Galatians 6:24),
- The flesh (Galatians 5:24, Romans 6: 6-7),
- The devil (Hebrews 2:14).

The past (2 Corinthians 5:14-17) which says, *"For the love of Christ controls us because we are convicted that one has died all; Therefore all have died…. Therefore if anyone is in Christ, he is a new creation, the old has passed away, behold the new has come"* (2 Corinthians 5: 14-17).

2. Renounce the things of darkness:

The work of the cross has to be individually appropriated for it to become effective in any life. It will remain ineffective until appropriated. The authority which the devil, the flesh, the world, the past have had on our minds must be deliberately denounced. We are not to break the power of these things. We cannot break down their powers. The cross had done that but we are to denounce that has been broken. *"We destroy arguments and every proud obstacle to he knowledge of God and take every thought captive to obey Christ"* (2 Corinthians 10:4).

This is possible because of the work on the cross. The cross enables us to come out from under the heaviest and most powerful mental bondage. The power of Satan, sin or habit cannot hold us captive any longer. We can be free from any moment we want. The door is opened out of the prison in which you are locked. Come out free. Come out now.

Make your act of renunciation specific, definite and whole-hearted. Confess it aloud until you and your confession become one. You can pray in the following lines: *"Satan, I renounced you and all your works. In the name of Jesus, I reject your hold on my mind because your authority was rendered null and void on the cross. I take back now, every inch of ground that I have yielded to you, and right now, I bring all my thoughts under the Lordship of Jesus Christ."*

You are free. If there are specific problems; an outstanding grudge, bitterness, any other thing they should be allowed to go and restitution carried out.

3. Receive The Gift Of A Renewed Mind:

The renewed mind is a gift. Receive it by faith expresses in prayer as you received the other gifts from the Lord, like salvation, healing, the baptism into the Holy Spirit and so on. Pray like this: *"Lord, I receive from Your hand now the gift of a renewed mind and thank You for it, in Jesus name"* Amen.

The result is peace and life because the conflicts have been resolved and then the peace of God becomes the guardian and the arbitrator. The Bible says, *"Have no anxiety about anything, but in everything by prayer and supplication with thanksgiving let your requests be made known to God. And the peace of God, which passes all understanding will keep your hearts and your minds in Christ Jesus"* (Philippians 4:6-7). *"Let the peace of Christ rule in your hearts, to which indeed you were called in the one body. And be thankful"* (Colossians 3:15).

This renewed mind is involved in the following:

1. Seeking the things that are above because it is a gift from above.

2. Is set on the things that are above because it is a gift from above.
3. Co-operates in putting to death what is earthly in you because it is not of earthly origin.
4. Co-operates in putting on the new nature because it is itself new.
5. It co-operates in putting on the new nature.
6. The peace of Christ rules in it.
7. It can receive the Word of Christ and co-operate to allow Christ to dwell richly in you.
8. It gives the truth and co-operates to ensure that you are taught and admonished in all wisdom.
9. It co-operates to ensure that you sing psalms and song unto the Lord.
10. It dwells on the things of the spirit.
11. It enables you to be a debtor to the Spirit.

The one in whom this mind fully operates is sanctified.

The mind, by being set on the right things, by being sensitive to the dictates of the peace of God within, and by walking in obedience, is maintained, renewed and the process of sanctification continues as the cross, in an increasing way, puts off all defeats in character, and the character of Christ in put on in a progressive way.

So the work of sanctification begins at conversion, is accelerated through the crises of knowing, reckoning, yielding, the operation of the law of the Spirit of life in Christ Jesus and the co-operation of the renewed mind and continues through all of life as Christ is formed in an increasing way in the believer and manifested in his character. We must fully co-operate to reach the highest level of sanctification possible.

All believers can be entirely sanctified if they want. That is, they can part with all the deeds of the flesh and be separated from the world. No believer can however reach the state of sanctification which Christ maintained for none can while on earth put one all of Christ:

perfect love

perfect peace

perfect joy

And rest, all the time as the Lord Jesus dis.

Yet, we must make this perfection our goal, for God who has called us is faithful and He will do it. When the Lord appears, our sanctification shall be fully fulfilled for we shall see Him and be like Him (1 John 3:12). *"And every one who thus hopes in him purifies himself even a he is pure"* (1 John 3: 2).

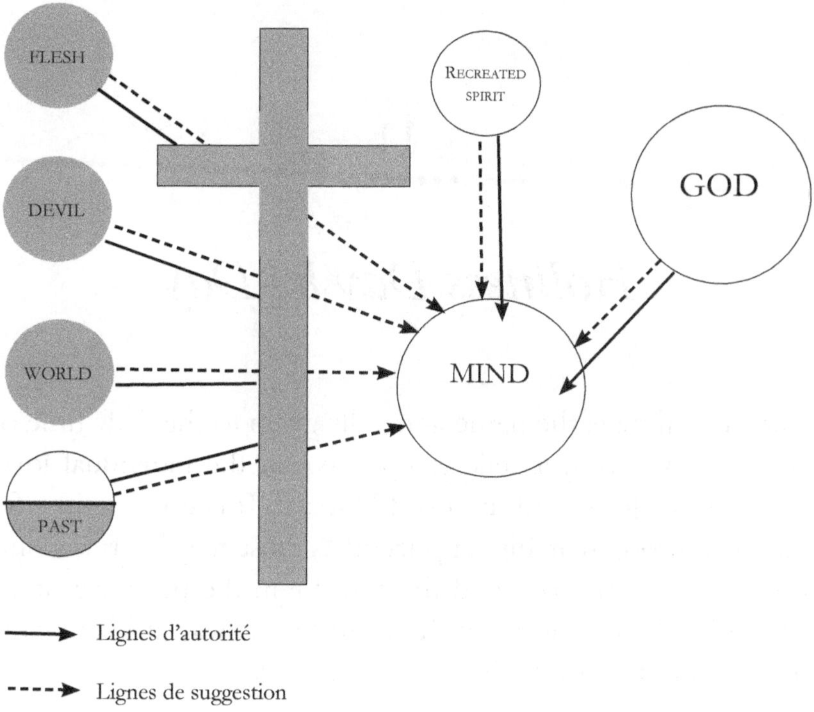

In the renewed mind, God and the recreated spirit have authority. The flesh, the devil, the world and the past have no authority whatsoever. They may nevertheless tempt (suggest) but their suggestions can always be rendered null and void by the renewed mind.

The renewed mind can thus remain untarnished all the time. In this limited sense someone can be said to be *"entirely sanctified"* but this is a limited sense. Entire sanctification must include total conformity to Christ in spinelessness and character.

11

Holiness Day by Day

The quiet time is the name generally given to the daily time of Bible study – prayer fellowship between the individual lover of the Lord Jesus and the Lord Himself. It is not the time for family or group worship, important as these may be. It is a one-tone affair – the Lord and the disciple in the presence of no one else. Those who meet the Lord in this way are kept close to Him and free from sin.

Mature saints, thought the years of this painful waiting for the clouds to open and reveal the Lord Jesus in person, have found this time when they can just fellowship wit their beloved Lord alone, indispensable for spiritual progress. I, too, have found that to true during the few years of my lonely pilgrimage in this dark and passing world.

Although the example of others is good, the supreme example is the Lord of glory Himself. The Bible says of Him; *"And in the morning, a great while before day, he rose and went out to a lonely place and there prayed"* (Mark 1:35). He did this habitually. He went away and was lost in God and lost with, so much that Simon and those who were with Him pursued Him, and when they found Him the said to Him Every one is searching for you."

Although Jesus is God and was always in vital fellowship with the Father, He nevertheless found it necessary to have that daily time of concentrated fellowship with His Father during which He renewed closest contact with Him, received from Him full approval for past actions and future plans as well as fresh anointing with power for the needs of that day.

May we notice that He spent a considerable amount of time with the Father, for He rose a great while before day. He enjoyed it so thoroughly that it needed Peter and the others to drag Him away from God's presence in that way. There were the pressing multitudes but the Lord knew that the time with the Father must take first place. He was not governed by circumstances but by a predetermined principle that He would not see the face of man before He had seen the face of the father; that He would not talk to man about the Father until He had to the Father about man.

He got His priorities right. No wonder His entire ministry was one story of unending success with the Father.

The Lord also sought a lonely place! The nature of the business with the Father was such that He could not transact it in the noise of a pressing world. He sought a place where He could have the fullest concentration, undisturbed by man and noise. We must make Him our example. If the Lord needed such a time, it is obvious that our need should be greater than His.

The Psalmist also found that He had to seek God first thing in the morning. The Bible says, *"O Lord, in the morning thou doest hear my voice; in the morning I prepare a sacrifice for thee and watch"* (Psalm 5:3); *"But I, O Lord, cry to thee, in the morning my prayer comes before thee"* (Psalm 88:13); *"I rise before dawn and cry for help; I hope in thy word"* (Psalm 119:147). I believe that it is imperative to seek God in the morning. If the purpose of seeking Him is partly to get clear directions for the day, then how can someone go out and mess the day up and then come at night to receive the instructions which he ought to have received in the morning? We live in days of gross indiscipline where even *"ministers"* of the gospel are gambling away the demands on the ministry of the altar of sleep, and many worship at the shrine of the goddess of indiscipline. We have not so learnt from the Lord, it is this, *"Awake, O sleeper, and arise from the dead, and Christ shall give you light"* (Ephesians 5:14).

This message is addressed to people who hunger for God; for people who seek Him. It is written for people who will not just go through the ritual of having had a quiet time but who will not depart from the Lord's presence until they have been touched by Him and have touched Him in return.

As a natural believer, I find two hours a basic time requirement for this time of Bible Study – prayer fellowship with the Lord. I strongly recommend those wonderful hours between 4.a.m. and 6.a.m. to be put aside for this business with God. The very young believer may have this need satisfied after a short time. The more mature will need more time. I consider this the number one business for the kingdom and invite you wholeheartedly to it.

You need a good Bible, a good note book, and a pen as basic material. God bless you richly.

"I acknowledge with profound gratitude that I used material from "THE HOUR THAT CHANGES THE WORLD" *(c) 1978 Baker House Grand Rapids in preparing the section on prayer in the Quiet Time"*

THE QUIET TIME - 1: BIBLE STUDY IN THE QUIET TIME

The Word of God is a revelation of the mind of God for His Body today. It is a love letter written by the Lord Jesus to His lovers. It will keep those who read it from sin. We have no choice about reading it. About the Word of God, Moses told Joshua, *"This book of the law shall not depart out of your mouth, but you shall meditate on it day and night, that you may be careful to do according to all that is written in it, for then you shall make your way prosperous, and then you shall have good success"* (Joshua 1:8). The Apostle Paul said, *"All Scripture is inspired by God and profitable for teaching, for proof, for correction, and for training in righteousness, that the man of God may be complete, equipped for every good work"* (2 Timothy 31-17).

The Following steps will help you during your Bible Study:

1. Thanksgiving for the Word:

We should start our Bible study with thanksgiving. Have you ever thought about the privilege that is ours of having the Word of God? See how available Bibles are in our land! We can have one version after the other. We can have commentaries, concordances and various Bible Study Aids. What a privilege! What a responsibility!! In Communities lands Bibles are rare. We ought to thank God for our spiritual privilege. In addition to thanking God for the availability of the Word, we are to thank God for the privilege of being able to read and write. Have you every thought about that? Please, thank God. Be grateful.

2. Ask God to Give you love for the Word:

We cannot make much out of the Word unless you we love and desire it. The Psalmist loved and desired God's Word. The Bible expressed it this way, *"The law of the Lord is perfect, reviving the soul…more to be desired are they than gold, even of the Lord is perfect, reviving the soul…more to be desired are they than gold, even 10).* "My soul is consumed with longing for thy ordinances at all time" *(Psalm119:20).* "At mid-night I rise to praise thee, because of thy righteous ordinances" *(Psalm119:62).* "The law of thy mouth is better to me than thousand of gold and silver pieces" *(Psalm119:72).* "Oh, how I love thy law! It is my meditation all the day" *(Psalm119: 97).* "How sweet are thy Word to my taste, sweeter than honey to my mouth" (Psalm119: 102).

My prayer to God is that He will yet raise in our generation men and women who, out of a pure heart will say with the Psalmist, *"Oh, how I love thy law,"* Only such will be at home with the Word. Only such will make the most of its inspired message. My beloved friend, ask God to create that desire in your heart for God's Word. Without it, your study will be cold, merely intellectual and you will not make much out of it. God will impart desire to those who truly seek Him ask Him.

3. Ask the Lord for spiritual understanding:

The Psalmist prayed and saint, *"Teach me, Oh Lord, the way of thy statutes; and I will keep it to the end. Give me understanding, that I may keep thy laws and observe it with my heart"* (Psalm119: 33-34). *"Open my eyes, that I may behold wondrous things out of thy law. I am a sojourner on earth; hide not thy commandments from me"* (Psalm119: 18-19). This desire for spiritual understanding, for revelation was not limited to David, the Psalmist. It was the prayer apostle Paul for the church. He put it this way, "For this reason because I have heard of your faith in the Lord Jesus and your love toward all the saints, I do not cease to give thanks for you, remembering you in my prayers, that the God of our Lord Jesus Christ, the Father of glory, may give you a spirit of wisdom and of revelation in the knowledge of Him, glory, may give you a spirit of wisdom and of revelation in the knowledge of Him, 23). Please read all of it many times over!!

So we need:

1. Spirit of wisdom

2. Spirit of revelation

3. Enlightenment of the eyes of our hearts so that we may know (i.e. understand, own, and use the spiritual knowledge that comes by revelation through the Word).

Why do need this work of the Holy Spirit in use we approach the Word? It is because of the ultimate purpose of the Word in us. The apostle prayed that this ultimate purpose of he Word might be realized. He said, *"For this reason I bow my knees before the Father, from whom every family in heaven and on earth is named, that according to the riches of His glory He may grant you to be strengthened with might through His spirit in the inner man, and that Christ may dwell in your hearts through faith; that you, being rooted and grounded in love, may have power to comprehend with all saints what is the breath and length and height and length and height and depth, and to know the love of Christ which surpasses knowledge, that you may be filled with the fullness of God"* (Ephesians 3:14-19).

What is the ultimate purpose of our Bible Study? It is to produce a people:

1. Strengthen in the inner man by the Holy Spirit.

2. Fully indwelt by Christ.

3. Rooted and grounded in the love of Christ with a capacity to understand, in the inner man, the limitless of that love.

4. To produce a person filled with the fullness of God.

So as you approach the Word, know that God has one purpose – to produce in you and out of you, a person *"filled with the fullness of God."* What a goal! What a possibility!!

4. Read The Passage

Now prepared for spiritual reception, you should read the passage of Scripture. As you read, mark out those areas, thoughts, phrases that speak to your heart at the first go. Jot them on paper on paper in your note (s) book and against them if need be.

5. Read The Passage Again:

Now, read the passage a second time to increase the areas that speak to your heart. If you can, you should read the passage from other translations of the Word; if possible read it from the Bible in another language. All these will help to make your understanding richer and to increase the spiritual impressions made on your spirit by the Holy Spirit through the Word.

6. Meditate On What Spoke To Your Heart:

Just close your eyes after reading over the things that God spoke to your heart and let the Word of Soak you. Sometimes the Word will minister to you in such a way that you will fell as if sweetness was being injected through you. At other times, you will fell such a sense of sinfulness and unworthiness that you would wish to run and be lost away from God's presence; Something akin to what Peter felt when he said, *"Depart from me O Lord, for I am a sinful man!"* Analyse what is making the impact on you. Ask the Lord to grant that the Word words of your mouth and the and the meditation of your heart may be accepted in His side. Speak out to God. Tell Him how you feel.

7. Riches To Keep – Spiritual Experience

Something will transpire between you and God as you meditate on His Word. You will see something of God – Father, Son and Holy Spirit, that you never saw before. Moses said to the Lord, *" I pray thee, show me thy glory"* (Exodus 33:18). The Lord did not reject that request. It was a holy desire and the Lord granted it. He said to him, *"I will make ALL my goodness pass before you…"* (Exodus 33:19). We must aim at spiritual experiences with God. We have Him and know Him in an increasing way until someday He too will make ALL of His goodness to pass before us.

Such experiences with God are rarely to be shared. We should store them. They are our private love-dealings with God and constitute something of our unexchangeable wealth. If we should share them too soon or carelessly, we shall suffer great loss. They are riches to keep.

8. Self-knowledge

One purpose of reading and studying the Word is that it may enable us to see ourselves as we are and not to be deceive by any other opinion we may like to build of ourselves. We can as, "What do I see of myself in the Word:

1. to thank God for? These include spiritual progress we have made, things that were problems to us I n the past that are no longer problems to us now because Christ has given us victory. We will also thank the Lord for an increasing vision of spiritual realities of an increasing love for the Lord and His body, and so on. Such items of thanksgiving should be written down not allowed off.

2. to repent of ? We should write down any sin that we have committed, confess it and claim deliverance from its power. There is no choice but to be specific with sin. There must be no general treatment of sin. Sin must be called sin – it must be specified and dealt with. Without this, spiritual progress is impossible; for how can God continue to reveal Himself to the one who harbours His greatest His greatest enemy, sin?

9 Obedience:

Unless the study of the Word has obedience in view, it is useless. The Psalmist said, *"Give me understanding, that I may KEEP thy law and observe it with my whole heart"* (Psalm 119:34). Total obedience is the one condition for continued fellowship with God. *"I will keep the law continually, for ever and ever"* (Psalm 119:44). *"Teach me, O Lord, the way of thy statutes; and I will keep it to the end"* (Psalm 119:32). *"The Lord is my portion; I promise to keep thy words"* (Psalm 119:57). The Lord demands obedience. The apostle James put it this way *"For if any is a hearer of the word and not a doer is like a man who observes his natural face in the mirror for he observes himself and goes away and at once forgets what he was like. But who he looks into the perfect law, the law of liberty, and persevere, being no hearer that forgets but a doer that act, he shall be blessed in the doing"* (James 1:23-25). Obedience is to God's negative command: *"thou shall not"* and to God's positive commands, *"thou shalt."* There has been an over-emphasis on what the believer is not to don. This has produced a withdrawn group of people with a negative type of Christianity. Such boast of what they do not do. I plead with you, my fellow saint, commit positive righteousness. Read and re-read the sermon on the mountain and you will see how Jesus viewed obedience.

Obedience!! Permit me to say this: The day must come in the life of the saint who is to mater with God when he willingly enrols as a student in the school of obedience – perfect obedience, unconditional obedience. The day must come when he obeys even the slightest promptings of the Holy Spirit.

From that day on, that one will never, never be the same again. From that day on, God would have acquired a choice verses and there can be no limits to the use of that vessel by God. From that day on, heaven would rejoice and hell would weep, for she would know that she could never make such a one disobey may command of God.

Dearest saint, have you enrolled in that school? Will you do so today? However, it is not simple words. Think and count the cost. Do not only think. Act! Commit yourself to a life of total obedience. That is God's best. It is also the best of you.

10. Riches to Store – Memorization:

The Psalmist said, *"I have laid up thy word I n my heart, that I might not sin against thee"* (Psalm 119:11). He memorized it. When the Lord was facing the severe battle with the Enemy in the wilderness, He quoted Scripture from memory. He said, *"It is written."* He had memorized at least a verse a day. In the passage you have been studying, there will be a verse that you want stored in your mind. Memorize it.

11. Riches to share:

The purpose of Bible study in the Quiet Time is to enrich oneself. However, this is not the end in itself, for the ultimate purpose of all spiritual knowledge is to build up the Body of Christ. We must do everything with the Body of Christ in view*"for the sake of the elect, that they also may obtain salvation in Christ Jesus with its eternal glory"* (2 Timothy 2:10). If we are to endure everything for the elect, then everything we do must be related to the whole Body. This means that I must think of the Body as I study the Word. It is useless jut to sending verses to people. That is very cheap things are of little value. I believe that the best way to approach it is to ask, *"What have I received as mine from the Lord to share with a member of the Body or with the assembly of the Body?"* The Lord may give you something to meet the need of a brother or a sister. Give him what you have received of the Lord for him. He may give you something for the local assembly. Look for the right opportunity to share it with the Body of Christ. You should be very clear before the Lord as for whom the word is meant. If say, the Lord sends you with a warning to a particular brother and you are careless enough to give that warning to another, you cause confusion that could have far-reaching consequences. Also, a message meant for an individual that is forgiven to the whole assembly also causes confusion. God is exact. He speaks clearly. Receive your message from Him. Know clearly for whom the message is meant, and deliver it with prayer that God will use it for spiritual blessing.

12. Praise and Thanksgiving:

The best place to stop our Bible study is with praise and thanksgiving. May we too, like the Psalmist say to the Lord, *"Accept my offerings of praise, O Lord"* (Psalm 119:108). We thank Him for touching us in a new way with His Word. We praise Him for new areas of truth revealed to us. We praise Him for His unchanging Word for He said, *"Heaven and earth will pass away, but my word will not pass away"* (Luke 21:33), and the Psalmist said, "For ever, O Lord, thy word is firmly fixed in the heaven' (Psalm 119: 98).

The quiet time - 2: Prayer in the quiet time

Bible Study in the Quiet Time should normally be followed by prayer. As we did with the Bible Study section, we shall divided this aspect of the Quiet Time into twelve small sections. You are not compelled to follow this order. Let the Holy lead you.

1. Praise, worship, adoration

Begin your prayer with time with worship and praise for the Lord inhabits the praise of His children. In praise, select the theme for your praise. Do not just throw words at God. Do not just say, *"I praise thee, I worship thee, I magnify thee, and so on."* You can do this for years and not grow in praise and if you were forbidden to use those words, you would be stranded. Psalm 150:1-2 gives us a good example. The Psalmist says, *"Praise him in his mighty firmament! Praise him for his mighty deeds; praise him according to his exceeding greatness."* So we are told to praise the Lord. We are told where to praise Him, and why to praise Him.

As you praise, concentrate on God and declare aloud all that God is and what He has done. Do not bring yourself into the picture. Forget yourself for a moment. We could follow the example, *"Make a joyful noise to God, all the earth; sing the glory of his name; give to Him glorious praise! Say to God,* "How terrible are thy deeds! So great is thy power that thy enemies cringe before thee. All the earth worship thee; they sing praise to thee, sing praises to thy name" (Psalm 66:1-4).

As you continue to praise, allow the Lord whom you are praising to reveal new themes of praise to you so that you will continually be growing in praise, worship and adoration.

2. Confession Of Sin:

Praise has brought us into vital contact with the Lord. If we are to continue in His presence, then all sin must go. This makes confession the obvious step to follow praise in our time of prayer. Here, stark honestly is requite. The Bible says, *"If we say that we have not sin, we deceive ourselves and the truth is not in us, but if we confess our sins, he is faithful and just to forgive us and cleanse us from all unrighteousness"* (1 John 1:8,9). So ask the Lord to search your heart for any unconfessed sin. The Psalmist expressed such a desire in the following words, *"O Lord thou hast searched me and know me! Thou knowest when I sit down and when I rise up; thou discerns my thoughts from afar. Thou searchest out my path and my lying down and art acquainted with all my ways. Even before a word is on my tongue. Lo, O lord, thou knowest it altogether"* (Psalm 139:1-4). Although God knows us so very thoroughly, we should still ask Him to search us. The Psalmist continue in the same Psalm to say *"search me O God, and know thy heart! Try me and know me in the way everlasting"* (Psalm 139:23,24).

Examine your recent activities to discover any area of failure, sin or compromise that needs confessing. Let the Lord examine your motives for all you have done in the recent past. Have the motive been pure? Let the Lord carefully weigh your motives! *"The Lord weighs the spirit"* (Proverbs 16:2). *"The Lord weighs the heart"* (Proverbs 21:2).

When the light of the Lord has shone into your heart to reveal the true condition of things, it will lead to confession. Confess all specific sins you may be guilty of either against God or against man. Confess sins that you have committed against the Body of Christ – pride, party spirit, refusal to co-operate for God's glory, a critical spirit and any others. Confess the grave sins of unbelief, doubt, laziness, lack of zeal, indiscipline, and so on. Confess your failure to love God supremely with *"all your heart and with all your soul, and with all your mind"* (Deuteronomy 6:5).

Also confess your need to be filled afresh with the Holy Spirit (Ephesians 5:15). God has promised to forgive, cleanse and forget. Claim those promises from Him. He says particularly to you, *"I will remember your sins and your misdeeds no more"* (See Hebrew 10:17). You are forgiven. You are pure. You can now go on into other areas of prayer-fellowship with God.

3. Waiting Upon The Lord

The purpose of waiting on the Lord is to enjoy Him early in your prayer-fellowship with Him. The Bible says, *"Wait for the Lord; be strong, and let your heart take courage, yea, wait for the Lord"* (Psalm 27:14). This is a command to be obeyed. *"Be still before the Lord and wait patiently for him"* (Psalm 37:7). The Lord says, *"Be still and know that I am God"* (Psalm 46:10). Such times of quiet waiting are dispensable for the growth of your spirit in the knowledge to God. They also justify the now Quiet Time, for it is principally a time of quiet before God.

As you enter into this sphere of your prayer-fellowship with God, bring your mind and spirit into a time of complete silence before the Lord. Cut off from the world completely. Think of no other though except thought of God – Father, Son and Holy Spirit. If you must say some something (I recommend no words whatsoever) whisper quietly, *"I love you Lord," "I miss You Lord", "I long for Your presence Lord", "Come soon Lord Jesus"* and any other words.

Concentrate on God's wondrous love for the world in general and for you in particular. Concentrate on His Being as the God of love, and expect something of His nature to *"flow"* into your being. *"Guard your steps when you go to the house of God, to draw near to listen is better than to offer the sacrifice of fools; for they do not know that they are doing evil. Be not rash with your mouth, nor let your heart be hasty to utter a word before God"* (Ecclesiastes 5:1-2).

4. Watching

The purpose of waiting is to become spiritually alert. The Bible says, *"Keep your heart with all vigilance"* (Proverbs 4:23). *"Watch and pray that you may not enter into temptation"*

Watch out the methods that Satan may be trying to use to hinder you from praying at the very moment, wandering thoughts, impure thoughts that suddenly flash from now where just to make you feel unworthy, restlessness, lack of concern in prayer, lack of a prayer burden, blankness, and many others.

Watch out for methods that Satan may be trying to use to hinder your walk with God, your work for the Lord, your spiritual ambitions. For example, he may bring thoughts of failure to discourage you and cause you to give up what you want to what you want to do for the Lord.

Watch out for ways that Satan may want to attack the local assembly, the work of the Lord in your town, area, country and world-wide.

Watching will make you now his devices. No that you know what the enemy what to do, destroys his plans in the name of the Lord. Claim the power and the victory of the Lord over Satan and his devices in all the areas above. Finally, claim the cover of the blood of the Lord over all these so that all his attempts would be futile.

5. Scripture praying

During your Bible Study, you found things in the Word to pray about and you wrote them down. This may include relations concerning the Lord, His Word, yourself, and so on. You may want to pray out the whole passage to the Lord or just a verse of it You may have been reading about Abraham's intercession for Sodom and you want to ask the Lord to make you into an effective intercessor. If you read about the need of labourers, you may want to obey the Lord's command and pray for labourers, just cover the lessons learnt in your study into prayer.

6. Intercession:

Intercessors are in higher demands. Sometimes the Lord looks out in vain for them. May God make you into an intercessor. Your intercession must be carefully planned. Make a list of topics of intercession. I suggest that that list should be include:

Your spiritual Leader (s). The ministry of the local church to which you belong. This should include your evangelism, her growth, her extensions, her maturation in love and unity, her ministry to backsliders, her ministry to the poor within and without, her ministry to the social needs of the community and others.

Intercede for the Word the gospel in your own, country, continent and world. For each place placed ask for more labourers for the over-ripped harvest. Ask for open doors for the gospel specially in countries where the doors are always closed or are closing. Ask the Lord to enable the gospel enterprise world-wide to produce abiding fruit and pray that funds will be available to meet needs of an expanding ministry.

Select a Moslem of Communist country, one per week and make it a subject of mighty intercession: that there would be a break through there for the gospel of our Blessed Lord.

7. Petition: asking for your needs

We have personal needs which we want to bring before the Lord. This is right and wholesome. During the time of petitions, we should begin by asking the Holy Spirit to guide our petitions so that we may claim only those things that will bring special honour to the Lord. We need to take James' warning seriously for he says, *"You ask and do not receive because you ask wrongly, to spend it on your passions"* (James 4:3). We are called to live here as pilgrims. Our lives must not betray any of the indulgences of those who are citizens of the perishing word.

1. Make a list of the specific needs you have for that day and present each need to the Lord.
2. Enlarge each request carefully taking time to explain to God why you desire and answer for that request. Stop and ask yourself. *"Is God convinced by my reasons or am I just trying to force it down His throat and thereby deceiving myself?"*
3. Quietly wait for the Lord to speak to you about these needs. He may reveal something you should do to have the answer to some need; He may assure you that the need has already been met or tell you that you should leave the matter with Him for He will attend to it in His own time.
4. Believe the Lord to supply all your needs and not wants. The Bible says, *"My God will supply every need of yours according to His riches in glory in Christ Jesus"* (Philippians 4:19). There is no need that He cannot meet. He will not withhold any good thing form those who walk uprightly" (Psalm 84:11).

5. Thank God for the answer to these needs that are coming. The Word of God says, ***"And this is the confidence we have in him, that if we ask anything according to his will he hears us. And if we know that he hears us in whatever we ask according to his will, we know that we have obtained the requests made of him"*** (1 John 5:14-15). Faith will pass into praise without waiting to see the answer. The Lord said, ***"Blessed are those who have not seed and yet believe"*** (John 20:29b). ***"Without faith it is impossible to please God"*** (Hebrews 11:6).

8. Listening to the Lord

You have just asked things from the Lord. While you were speaking, God was listening to you. Now, you listen to Him talk to you. He may ask you questions concerning the petitions that you made. Answer Him. He may ask you to explain in detail. Please explain. He may make His requests on your life, time, money and so on. Answer Him. He may reveal a need that you did not know that you had and promise to meet it for you so as to increase your joy. He may make you know Him in some additional way. He may give you a new spiritual gift. He may give you very specific instructions like: witness to this person; pray for that person; give the sum of X francs to that brother whom I will send to you; sister X will come to you with a need but you must do nothing about it for I have others plans about meeting her need; brother Y needs a word of encouragement. His problem is …… Take this word of encouragement to him at once.

As the Lord is speaking and you are listening, write down what He is saying. If He is giving exact, detailed instructions, then He means you to carry them out with the same degree of exactitude.

Sometimes you may hear the Lord saying, *"I want you to go on a fast for three days in order to pure life into my local body."* You should then ask the Lord when the fast should begin and He will tell you.

There is no limit to what the Lord will say to the waiting, listening saint. I can only say with certainty that the Lord will speak to His children who desire Him, who are pure and close to Him.

9. Meditation

God has just spoken to you during your time of listening. Meditate on the things that He said that He said to you. Ask questions to Him that He will make your obedience easier. Fir example, If He asked you to give someone something and you do not have the thing to him, you simply ask, *"Lord, how am I to obtain the money to give that brother?"*

In meditation, you are caught up in wonder at so great a God talking to you. So often, meditation will be short because you cannot help but burst into:

10. Singing.

Singing is the normal lot of Spirit-filled people. The Bible commands that we sing to the Lord. *"Sing praises to him, tell of all his wonderful works"* (1 Chronicles 16:9). *"I will sing praise to the God of Jacob"* (Psalm 75:9). *"Sing aloud to God our strength; shout for joy to the God of Jacob"* (Psalm 81:1).

You should stop for some time during your prayer fellowship with the Lord to sing a song of praise or adoration to Him. You can begin by singing the song that spontaneously comes from your being tot eh Lord or you can choose a particular hymn from a hymn book, with a particular theme and sing to Him.

You can also sing a new song to the Lord. The Bible says, *"Sing to the Lord a new song, his praises from the end of the earth"* (Isaiah 42:10). We are further commanded, *"Sing to Him a new song"* (Psalm 33:3). "He put a new song in my mouth, a song of praise to our God. Many will see and fear, and put their trust in the Lord (Psalm 40:3). This new song can come in many ways, including a Bible passage that the Lord enables you to transform into a song or a song which you compose and sing to the Lord or Spirit's specific impartation to your spirit.

In addition to these new songs in known language, the Lord may give you a song in n unknown tongue to sing to Him. In fact this ought to be normal. The apostle Paul said, *"For if I pray in a tongue, my spirit prays but my mind is unfruitful. What am I to do? I will pray with the spirit and I will pray with the mind also"* (I Corinthians 14:14,15).

The best songs at this stage in our prayer-fellowship are songs of worship and adoration. Singing produces worship in heaven. It will do the same on earth. The Bible says, *"And they sang a new song, saying; worthy art thou to take the scroll and to open its seals, for thou wast slain and by thy blood didst ransom men for God, from every tribe and tongue and people and nation and hast made them a kingdom and priest to our God, and they shall reign on earth. Then I looked and I heard around the throne and the living creatures and the elders the voice of many angels, numbering myriads of myriads of thousands, saying with a loud voice,* "Worthy is the Lam who was slain, to receive power and wealth and wisdom and might and honour and glory and blessing!" *And I heard every creature in heaven and on earth and under the earth and in the sea, and all therein, saying,* "To him who sits upon the throne and the Lamb be blessing and honour and glory and might for ever and ever! And the four living creatures said, *"Amen"* and the elders fell down and worship" (Revelation 5:9-14). To best of my understanding, this is the most far-reaching worship in all of scriptures, involving as it were the largest number and variety of creatures. Yet it is most interceding to note that that, that far- reaching praise was triggered by a new song. What mighty worship could your own new song produce? It could trigger events of every far- reaching consequences for the Lord our God. Glory be to His Holy Name!

11. Thanksgiving

Singing should give place naturally to thanksgiving. Ask the Lord to open your eyes so that you may see how good He has been to you. Count your blessings, name them one by one. I recommend that you should keep a written record of all blessings you receive from the Lord day by day. Begin with your blessings that the Lord has bestowed upon you in recent days.

1. Spiritual blessings- growth in the Lord, new revelations of the Lord, new babies born into the Kingdom, victory over besetting sins, and so on.
2. Material blessings – food, shelter, clothes, money, gifts received, etc. Also thank the Lord for health, protection friends, loved ones, and so on.

Thank the Lord for blessings that you expect to receive from Him in the future. Also thank the Lord for at least one blessing which you have never thanked Him for. Nothing pleases the Lord more than thanksgiving from Him children. Ingratitude, so prevalent even among believers is a terrible sin. The Lord says, *"He who brings thanksgiving as his sacrifice honours me"* (Psalm 50:23). Should we not respond to saying, *"I will offer to thee the sacrifice of thanksgiving?"* (Psalm 116:17). We should.

I further recommend that there should be seasons of thanksgiving – particular periods when all of our fellowship is cantered on thanksgivings. Such seasons can only make us richer in our fellowship with Him.

12. Praise

The best note on which to end our fellowship with the Lord is in praise. Praise Him for who He is – a personal Friend. Praise Him for all that has transpired between you and Him during your Quiet Time. Confess aloud that you love Him, that you have faith in Him, that you believe His Word and that you are victorious in Christ Jesus. This is wonderful. It satisfies Him and you go away truly blessed and yearn for the nest time that you will be privileged to spend such glorious times in His presence.

1. *Sweet hour of prayer, sweet hour of prayer,*
   That calls me from a world of care
   And bids me at my Father's throne Makes all my wants and wishes known; In seasons of distress and grief,
   My soul has often found relief,
   And oft escaped the tempter's snare, By thy return, sweet hour of prayer.

2. *Sweet hour of prayer, sweet hour of prayer, Thy wings shall my petition bear,*

To Him whose truth and faithfulness Engage the waiting soul to bless;

And since He bids me seek His face, Believe His Word and trust His grace, I'll cast on Him my every care,

And wait for thee, sweet hour of prayer.

3. *Sweet hour of prayer, sweet hour of prayer, May I thy consolation share,*

   Till, from Mount Pisgah's lofty height I view my home, and take my flight:

   This robe of flesh I'll drop and rise To seize the everlasting prize;

   And shout while passing through the air Farewell, Farewell, sweet hour of prayer!

W.W. Walford.

Very important

If you have not yet received Jesus as your Lord and Saviour, I encourage you to receive Him. Here are some steps to help you,

Admit that you are a sinner by nature and by practice and that on your own you are without hope. Tell God you have personally sinned against Him in your thoughts, words and deeds. Confess your sins to Him, one after another in a sincere prayer. Do not leave out any sins that you can remember. Truly turn from your sinful ways and abandon them. If you stole, steal no more. If you have been committing adultery or fornication, stop it. God will not forgive you if you have no desire to stop sinning in all areas of your life, but if you are sincere, He will give you the power to stop sinning.

Believe that Jesus Christ, who is God's Son, is the only Way, the only Truth and the only Life. Jesus said, «*I am the way, the truth and the life; no one comes to the Father, but by me*» (John 14:6). The Bible says, «*For there is one God, and there is one mediator between God and men, the man Christ Jesus, who gave himself as a ransom for all*» (1 Timothy 2:5-6). «*And there is salvation in no one else (apart from Jesus), for there is no other name under heaven given among men by which we must be saved*» (Acts 4:12). «*But to all who received him, who believed in his name, he gave power to become children of God...*» (John 1:12). But,

CONSIDER the cost of following Him. Jesus said that all who follow Him must deny themselves, and this includes selfish financial, social and other interests. He also wants His followers to take up their crosses and follow Him. Are you prepared to abandon your own interests daily for those of Christ? Are you prepared to be led in a new direction by Him? Are you prepared to suffer for Him and die for Him if need be? Jesus will have nothing to do with half-hearted people. His demands are total. He will only receive and forgive those who are prepared to follow Him AT ANY COST. Think about it and count the cost. If you are prepared to follow Him, come what may, then there is something to do.

INVITE Jesus to come into your heart and life. He says, «*Behold I stand at the door and knock. If anyone hears my voice and opens the door (to his heart and life), I will come in to him and eat with him, and he with me* « (Revelation 3:20). Why don't you pray a prayer like the following one or one of your own construction as the Holy Spirit leads ?

> «Lord Jesus, I am a wretched, lost sinner who has sinned in thought, word and deed. Forgive all my sins and cleanse me. Receive me, Saviour and transform me into a child of God. Come into my heart now and give me eternal life right now. I will follow you at all costs, trusting the Holy Spirit to give me all the power I need.»

When you pray this prayer sincerely, Jesus answers at once

and justifies you before God and makes you His child.

Please write to me and I will pray for you and help you as you go on with Jesus Christ...

If you have received the Lord Jesus-Christ after reading this book, please write to us at the following addresse :

For Europe :

Editions du Livre Chrétien

4, Rue du Révérend Père Cloarec

92400 Courbevoie

Courriel : editionlivrechretien@gmail.com

TRUE CONVERSION (MARK 10:17-31)

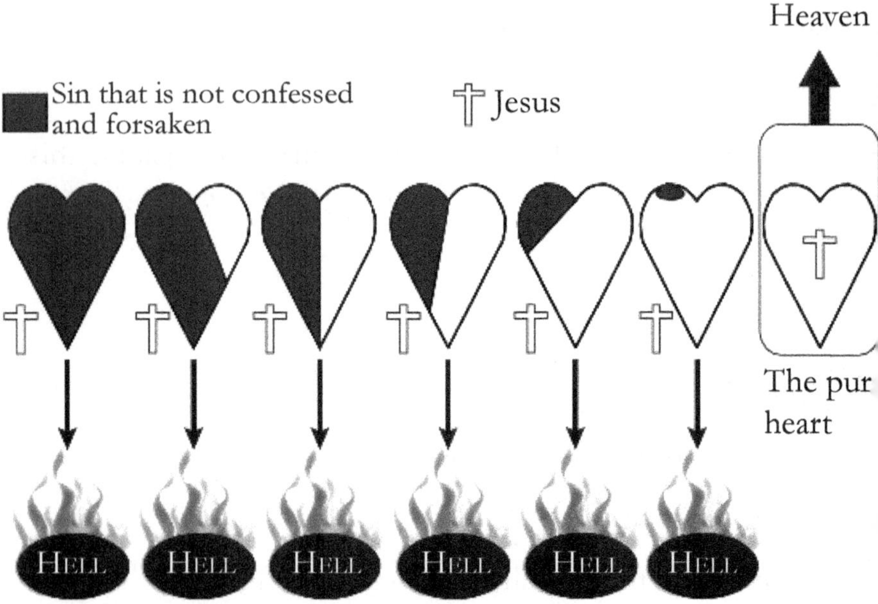

All the blemished hearts represent unsaved persons. The last pure heart alone represents the saved person.

Jesus cannot come in to blot out some of a person's sins and not others. He comes in to blot out all sins or no sin at all.

He blots out sin that is confessed and forsaken forever.

He comes in to be Saviour, Lord and King in all things and in all circumstances or He does not come in at all.

He cannot come in to be Saviour without being Lord and King because He cannot divide Himself. He is Saviour, Lord and King of all or Saviour, Lord and King of nothing at all.

Professor Zacharias Tanee Fomum

About the author

Professor Z.T. Fomum was born in 1945 in Cameroon and was taken to be with the Lord on the 14th March 2009. He was admitted to the Bachelor of Science degree, graduating as a prize-winning student from Fourah Bay College in the University of Sierra Leone. His research in Organic Chemistry earned him a Ph.D. degree in the University of Makerere, Kampala, Uganda. Recently, his published scientific work was evaluated and found to be of high distinction, earning him the award of a Doctor of Science degree from the University of Durham in Great Britain. As a Professor of Organic Chemistry in the University of Yaoundé I, Cameroon, he supervised and co-supervised more than 100 Master's and Doctoral degree theses. He published with others over 160 scientific articles in leading international journals.

The author read over 1350 books on the Christian Faith and wrote over 150 titles to advance the Gospel of Christ. 4 million copies of these books are in circulation in 11 languages, as well as 16 million gospel tracts in 17 languages. In pursuance of the purpose to proclaim the Gospel of Jesus Christ, he also made a total of over 700 missionary journeys in Cameroon and over 500 in 70 nations. These ranged from 2 days to 6 weeks in all the world's six continents.

The author led a Church-planting and missionary-sending movement, by whose ministrations, more than 10,000 healing miracles were performed by God in answer to prayer in the name of Jesus. These miracles include instant healings of; headaches, cancers, HIV/AIDS, blindness, deafness, dumbness, paralysis, madness and diverse diseases.

The author was married to Prisca Zei Fomum and they had 7 children who are all actively involved in serving the Lord. Prisca is a national and international minister specialising in the winning and discipling of children to Jesus Christ. She also communicates and imparts the vision of the ministry to children, with a view to raise and build up ministers for them.

The author owed all that he was and all that God had done in him and through him, to the unmerited favours and blessings of God and to his world wide army of friends and co-workers. He considered himself nothing without them and the blessings of God, and would have amounted to nothing but for them.

May the Lord receive all the glory!

OTHERS BOOKS BY ZACHARIAS TANEE FOMUM

- THE CHRISTIAN WAY
- The way of life
- The way of obedience
- The way of discipleship
- The way of sanctification
- The way of Christian character
- The way of spiritual power
- The way of Christian service
- The way of spiritual warfare
- The way of overcomers
- The way of suffering for Christ
- The way of spiritual encouragement
- The way of loving the Lord
- The way of victorious praying

-

- THE PRAYER
- The ministry of fasting
- The art of intercession
- The practice of intercession
- Praying with power
- Practical spiritual warfare through prayer
- Moving God through prayer
- The ministry of praise and thanksgiving
- Waiting on the Lord in prayer
- The ministry of supplication
- Life-changing thoughts on prayer, Vol 1
- Life-changing thoughts on prayer, Vol 2
- Life-changing thoughts on prayer, Vol 3
- The centrality of prayer

-

- PRACTICAL HELPS FOR OVERCOMERS
- The use of time
- Retreats for spiritual progress
- Personal spiritual revival
- Daily dynamic encounters with God
- The school of truth
- How to succeed in the Christian life
- The Christian and money
- Deliverance from the sin of laziness
- The art of working hard
- Knowing God – The greatest need of the hour
- Restitution : An important message for the overcomers
- Revelation a must
- True repentance
- You can receive a pure heart today
- You can lead someone to the Lord Jesus today
- The overcomer as a servant of man
- You have a talent!
- The Making of Disciples
- The secret of spiritual fruitfulness
- The dignity of manual labour

-

- GOD, SEX AND YOU
- Enjoying the premarital life
- Enjoying the choice of your marriage partner
- Enjoying the married life
- Divorce and remarriage
- A successful marriage; the husband's making
- A successful marriage; the wife's making

-

- EVANGELISATION
- God's love and forgiveness
- Come back home my son; I still love you
- Jesus loves you and wants to heal you
- Come and see; Jesus has not changed!
- 36 reasons for winning the lost to Christ
- Soul winning, Volume 1
- Soulwinning, Volume 2
- Celebrity a mask

-

- MAKING SPIRITUAL PROGRESS

- Vision, burden, action
- The ministers and the ministry of the new covenant
- The cross in the life and ministry of the believer
- Knowing the God of unparalleled goodness
- Brokenness, the secret of spiritual overflow
- The secret of spiritual rest
- Making spiritual progress, Volume 1
- Making spiritual progress, Volume 2
- Making spiritual progress, Volume 3
- Making spiritual progress, Volume 4

-

- PRACTICAL HELPS IN SANCTIFICATION

- Deliverance from sin
- Sanctified and consecrated for spiritual ministry
- The Sower, the seed and the hearts of men
- Freedom from the sin of adultery and fornication
- The sin before you may lead to immediate death: Do not commit it!
- Be filled with the Holy Spirit
- The power of the Holy Spirit in the winning of the lost

-

- OTHER BOOKS

- Are you still a disciple of the Lord Jesus?
- A broken vessel
- The joy of begging to belong to the Lord Jesus : A testimony
- Laws of spiritual success, Volume 1
- Discipleship at any cost
- The shepherd and the flock
- Spiritual aggressiveness
- The secluded worshipper
- Deliverance from demons
- Inner healing
- No failure needs to be final
- You can receive the baptism into the Holy Spirit now
- Facing life's problems victoriously
- A word to the students
- The prophecy of the overthrow of the satanic prince of Cameroon
- The power to operate miracles

-

- NEW BOOKS

- Church Planting Strategies
- Delivrance from the Sin Of The Gluttony
- God Centredness
- God, Money And You
- In The Crucible For Service
- Issues Of The Heart
- Jesus Saves And Heals Today
- Leading A Local Church
- Meet The Liberator
- Power For Service
- Prayer And A Walk With God
- Prayer crusade Volume 1
- Revolutionary Thoughts On Spiritual Leadership
- Roots And Destinies
- Spiritual Fragrange
- Spiritual Gifts
- Spiritual Nobility
- The Art Of Worship
- The Believer's Conscience
- The Character And Personality Of The Leader
- The Leader & His God
- The Overthrow Of Principalities And Powers
- The Processes Of Faith
- The Spirit Filled Life
- Victorious Dispositions
- Walking With God
- Women Of The Glory Vol 1
- Women Of The Glory Vol 2
- Women Of The Glory Vol 3
- You, Your Team And Your Ministry